D0455835

HBR Guide to
Managing Stress at Work

HARVARD BUSINESS REVIEW PRESS

Boston, Massachusetts

Library of Congress Cataloging-in-Publication Data

HBR guide to managing stress at work.
    pages cm
  Includes index.
  ISBN 978-1-4221-9601-4 (alk. paper)
1. Job stress.   I. Harvard business review.
  HF5548.85.H42 2013
  158.7'2—dc23

                    2013033054

HBR Guide to
Managing Stress at Work

Harvard Business Review Guides

Arm yourself with the advice you need to succeed on the job, from the most trusted brand in business. Packed with how-to essentials from leading experts, the HBR Guides provide smart answers to your most pressing work challenges.

The titles include:

HBR Guide to Better Business Writing

HBR Guide to Finance Basics for Managers

HBR Guide to Getting the Mentoring You Need

HBR Guide to Getting the Right Job

HBR Guide to Getting the Right Work Done

HBR Guide to Giving Effective Feedback

HBR Guide to Making Every Meeting Matter

HBR Guide to Managing Stress at Work

HBR Guide to Managing Up and Across

HBR Guide to Persuasive Presentations

HBR Guide to Project Management

What You'll Learn

Struggling to keep up with your many commitments? Feeling snappish? Unable to sleep? You're painfully familiar with the signs of work-related stress—chronic headaches, impatience with colleagues and family, loss of focus, fluctuating weight, nails bitten to the quick. And you know what you're supposed to do to prevent them: Stick to your priorities. Work more efficiently. Get adequate sleep. Exercise regularly. Limit your caffeine. But sometimes, when the pressure's on, all that is easier said than done. You shortchange yourself to meet a tight deadline or win a new client.

True, a certain amount of stress boosts your productivity. But then you push it too far, and it saps your energy and performance.

How do you put yourself on an even keel—and stay there? This guide will give you the tools you need to do your best work by protecting and feeding your well-being.

You'll learn how to:

- Harness stress so that it spurs your productivity

- Create realistic, sustainable rituals

- Aim for progress, not perfection

- Make a case for a flexible schedule

- Decide when to set work/life boundaries and when to blur them

- Leave a bad day at the office *at the office*

- Ease the physical tension of spending too much time at your computer

- Manage a dual-career relationship

- Renew yourself physically, mentally, and emotionally

Contents

Contents

Section 4: FINDING THE TOOLS THAT WORK FOR YOU

Introduction: Nine Ways Successful People Defeat Stress

by Heidi Grant Halvorson

Feeling stressed? Of course you are. You have too much on your plate, deadlines looming, and people counting on you. You're under a lot of pressure—so much that, at times, the quality of your work suffers.

But overall, your success on the job doesn't depend on *whether* you suffer from intense bouts of stress. These days, nearly all professionals do. What matters is *how you deal with them.* When your stress levels get out of hand, these nine methods will help you regain balance.

Adapted from content posted on hbr.org on December 13, 2012

1. Cut Yourself Some Slack

When you're feeling overwhelmed, dwelling on your failures and weaknesses won't solve the problem. You're better off looking at your mistakes with compassion and remembering that everyone messes up now and then. Research shows that people who do this aren't just happier, more optimistic, and less anxious and depressed—they're also more successful. In one study, Berkeley's Juliana Breines and Serena Chen gave people who had failed a test a chance to retake it and improve their scores. Those with a self-compassionate view of their failure studied 25% longer and scored higher on the second test than participants who weren't self-compassionate.

Most of us believe we need to be hard on ourselves to perform at our best. But by giving yourself permission to make mistakes and learn from them, you can actually reduce your stress *and* improve your performance.

2. See the Big Picture

As you're facing your mountain of tasks, draw energy and motivation from the larger goals you're striving for. By thinking about the greater purpose that each action supports, you'll cast a whole new light on things that don't seem important or inspiring on their own. Next time you're slogging through e-mails at the end of a long day, don't think of it as merely "digging myself out of my inbox." View it as "wrapping up a critical project on schedule," for example, or "showing decision makers how committed I am to meeting their goals." Studies show that when we think about the *why* behind our behavior, we're less impulsive, less vulnerable to temptation, and more likely to plan our actions in advance. We're more certain of who we are and what we want, and we're therefore much less likely to feel that outside forces—such as other people, luck, or fate—control what happens to us.

3. Rely on Routines

If I asked you to name the major causes of stress in your work life, you'd probably cite deadlines, time-sucking meetings, a heavy workload, bureaucracy, and maybe even a controlling boss. You might not think to say "making decisions," because most of us aren't aware of this powerful and pervasive cause of stress in our lives. Yet every time you make a decision—which candidate to hire, when to ask your supervisor for help, whether to delegate a task— you create mental tension that is, in fact, stressful.

So use routines to reduce the number of decisions you need to make. U.S. President Barack Obama, who has one of the most stressful jobs imaginable, takes this approach. Here's what he told *Vanity Fair* (October 2012) about it:

> *You'll see I wear only gray or blue suits. I'm trying to pare down decisions. I don't want to make decisions about what I'm eating or wearing. Because I have too many other decisions to make. You need to focus your decision-making energy. You need to routinize yourself. You can't be going through the day distracted by trivia.*

If there's something you need to do every day, do it *at the same time* every day. Establish a ritual for preparing for work in the morning, for example: Perhaps you can check e-mails and voice mails and respond to the urgent ones first thing, which clears the decks and makes it easier to move more quickly to important projects. Set up a similar routine for packing up to go home at night. Once you've put less-important decisions on autopilot, they'll stop weighing on you—and you'll free up your energy for things that matter more.

4. Do Something Interesting

Interest in an activity doesn't just keep you going despite fatigue—it actually *replenishes* your energy for whatever you'll do next. That's what Dustin Thoman (California State University), Jessi Smith (Montana State University), and Paul Silvia (University of North Carolina at Greensboro) learned in a recent experiment: They gave participants a particularly draining task and then varied whether the *next* task was difficult but interesting or relatively easy but dull. The people who received the harder follow-up task put in more effort and performed much better—despite being tired—than those who worked on the easy one. Engagement restored their energy.

In another study, the researchers found that interest resulted in better performance on a *subsequent* task as well. In other words, you won't just do a better job on Task A because you find Task A interesting—you'll do a better job on follow-up Task B *because you found Task A interesting.* The replenished energy flows into whatever you do next. So make time during your day for projects that fascinate you, for brainstorming, and for reading about exciting innovations in your field. All that will help you power through your less-interesting but necessary tasks. (You'll find more examples and ideas in section 2, "Renewing Your Energy.") Also, remember that *interesting* doesn't merely mean pleasant, fun, or relaxing. As the studies cited above show, it's something that captivates you and requires effort.

5. Add *When* and *Where* to Your To-Do List

Does a whole day (or even a week) often go by before you check a single item off your lengthy to-do list? Stressful, isn't it?

To get things done in a timely manner, add a specific *when* and *where* to each task on your list. If-then planning can help you fill in those blanks. For example, "Call Bob" becomes "*If* it's Tuesday after lunch [when], *then* I'll call Bob from my desk [where]." Now that you've created an if-then plan for calling Bob, your unconscious brain will start scanning the environment, searching for the conditions in the *if* part of your plan. This enables you to seize the critical moment and make the call, even when you're busy doing other things. You've already done the hard work of deciding what to do; now you can execute the plan without consciously thinking about it.

Nearly 200 studies, on everything from negotiation and time management to diet and exercise, show that deciding in advance when and where you will complete a task can double or triple your chances of actually doing it. Bracing yourself for an upcoming presentation? Don't just fret about it—make a date with yourself to prepare: "*If* I can reserve a small conference room [where] for an hour tomorrow afternoon [when], *then* I'll use it to practice going through my slides."

6. Articulate Your Desired Response

When we're stressed, it can feel as if the universe is conspiring against us. It's easy to get trapped in a negative spiral, ruminating on everything that's going wrong—essentially paralyzing ourselves. Perfectionism can similarly trap us. We keep going into the weeds to fix "just one more thing." Projects never get done because we're endlessly fiddling with them.

How do you break the cycle when it's your own mind playing tricks on you? Do some additional if-then planning, because it can help you do more than tackle your to-dos. According to research by NYU's Peter Gollwitzer, it also allows you to control emotional responses such as fear, sadness, fatigue, self-doubt, and even disgust. Just think of the situations that provoke those reactions from you and decide how you would like to respond instead. Then make an if-then plan that links your desired response to the situations that tend to raise your blood pressure. For instance: "*If* I see lots of e-mails in my inbox when I log in, *then* I will take three deep breaths to stay calm and relaxed." Whatever thoughts or actions work for *you*, make them a part of your if-then plan.

7. Focus on Improving, Not Perfecting

We all pursue our goals with one of two mind-sets: what I call the *be-good approach,* where you focus on proving that you already know what you're doing, and the *get-*

better approach, where you concentrate on developing your abilities and learning new skills. It's the difference between wanting to show that you *are smart* and wanting to *get smarter.*

If you're in be-good mode, expecting to do everything perfectly right out of the gate, you may constantly (often unconsciously) compare yourself with others to see how you size up. And when things don't go smoothly, you'll quickly start to doubt the abilities you're desperately trying to prove, which creates more stress and anxiety. Ironically, worrying about your ability makes you much more likely to fail.

A get-better mind-set, by contrast, leads to *self-*comparison: You measure how well you're doing today against how you did yesterday, last month, or last year. When you catch yourself comparing your performance with others' or being too self-critical, shift your perspective by asking yourself "Am I improving?" (and "If I'm not, what can I do to change that?"). You'll experience far less stress—and it will be easier to stay motivated, despite any setbacks.

8. Appreciate the Progress That You've Already Made

"Of all the things that can boost emotions, motivation, and perceptions during a workday, the single most important is making progress in meaningful work." That's the central idea in Teresa Amabile and Steven Kramer's book *The Progress Principle.* They argue that it's the "small wins" that keep us going—particularly in the face of stressors.

So it's enormously helpful to reflect on what you've accomplished so far before turning your attention to the challenges that remain ahead. If you're stressed by a complex yearlong project six months in, take a moment to list what's been done since day 1. Remember the difficulties you've already encountered and how you dealt with them. Then, with a sense of well-earned confidence, think about how far you have left to go and keep your eyes on the prize.

9. Know What Motivates You

Without realizing it, we can add stress to our work lives by managing it in ways that don't mesh with our own motivational styles. Figuring out what drives you will help you rein in your stress.

If it's optimism, you have what psychologists call a *promotion focus*: You think of your job as rife with opportunities for achievement. You're driven by the belief that everything will work out if you apply yourself. You probably also:

- Work quickly

- Brainstorm lots of alternatives to consider

- Plan for best-case scenarios

- Seek positive feedback (and lose steam without it)

- Feel dejected when things go wrong

The best way to cope with your stress is to maintain forward momentum. Motivation feels like eagerness to you—it runs on positivity. If you're feeling stuck, shift to another project and make some progress there before returning to the original obstacle. Also, since you're someone who needs to stay optimistic to be truly effective, reflect on some of your past triumphs to keep your chin up.

By contrast, if you have a *prevention focus,* you're motivated by security—and hanging on to what you've worked so hard for. You tend to:

- Work deliberately, with a high degree of accuracy

- Prepare yourself for the worst

- Get stressed over short deadlines

- Stick to tried-and-true ways of doing things

- Feel uncomfortable with praise or optimism

- Get anxious when things go wrong

For you, managing stress at work largely means avoiding mishaps and fulfilling your responsibilities. It feels like vigilance, and it's sustained by a kind of defensive pessimism—the need to keep danger at bay. In fact, it feels downright *wrong* to "stay positive" when you're under stress. You actually work best when you think about what might go awry and what you can do to keep that from happening (or how you'll respond if it happens, anyway). When you're dealing with potential budget cuts, for example, you cope most effectively by preempting the problem—figuring out where you can trim some of the fat, just in case. To others, this might seem like wallowing in negativity and making your life needlessly stressful (after all, the budget cuts might not happen), but you're actually alleviating stress by considering all possible scenarios and solutions and planning accordingly. You're working to minimize your losses.

We all take different views (promotion versus prevention) at different times, depending on which challenges we're facing. But most of us have a dominant motivational style. Identify yours, and then embrace either the sunny outlook or the hearty skepticism that will reduce your stress and keep you performing at your best.

The nine ideas I've shared here are just a start. You'll find many other useful tips in this guide—practical advice from experts on how to balance work and family, how to refill your tank when you're running on fumes, and tools to use when you're completely overwhelmed. If you're currently under a lot of pressure, you may want to skip ahead to section 4, "Finding the Tools That Work for You."

Here's the main thing to remember as you read: When it comes to stress, you are far from powerless. You may not be able to remove the stressors from your life, but you can take control of how they affect you. Stress doesn't have to interfere with your productivity, your health, and your happiness. You can even learn to harness its power for good by viewing stress-inducing challenges as opportunities to become more skilled and resilient.

Heidi Grant Halvorson is associate director for the Motivation Science Center at Columbia Business School. She's the author of *Nine Things Successful People Do Differently* (Harvard Business Review Press, 2012) and *Focus: Use Different Ways of Seeing the World for Success and Influence* (Hudson Street Press, 2013). Follow her on Twitter: @hghalvorson.

Section 1
Understanding How You're Wired

Chapter 1
Are You Working Too Hard?

A Conversation with Herbert Benson, MD

by Bronwyn Fryer

A summary of the full-length HBR interview with **Herbert Benson, MD,** *highlighting key ideas.*

THE IDEA IN BRIEF

The key to overcoming negative stressors is the *breakout principle,* or relaxing at the height of your struggle. There are four steps:

Adapted from *Harvard Business Review,* November 2005 (product #R0511B)

1. Take on a thorny problem, and really work hard at it until you feel you have reached the limits of your performance.

2. Walk away. Do something entirely different, such as breathing deeply while focusing on a calm phrase or taking a nap or hot shower.

3. Let go. This is the actual breakout, where you experience a flow of creative ideas and solutions.

4. Return to the "new-normal" sense of self-confidence.

Do the breakout sequence whenever you need to—and achieve gains in productivity and success.

When does stress help your performance, and when does it hurt? To find out, HBR senior editor Bronwyn Fryer talked with Herbert Benson, MD, founder of the Mind/Body Medical Institute in Chestnut Hill, Massachusetts. Also an associate professor of medicine at Harvard Medical School, Benson has spent more than 35 years conducting research in the fields of neuroscience and stress. He is best known for his 1975 best-seller, *The Relaxation Response.* He first described a technique to bring forth the complex physiological dance between stress and relaxation, and the benefits to managers of practices such as meditation, in "Your Innate Asset for Combating Stress" (HBR July–August 1974). His most recent book is *Relaxation Revolution* (Scribner, 2011) with William Proctor.

Benson and Proctor have found that we can learn to use stress productively by applying the *breakout principle*—a paradoxical active-passive dynamic. By using simple techniques to regulate the amounts of stress we feel, we can increase performance and productivity and avoid burnout. In this edited conversation, Benson describes how we can tap into our own creative insights, boost our productivity at work, and help our teams do the same. He is quick to acknowledge the large part Proctor's thinking has played in the ideas he discusses here.

HBR: We all know that unmanaged stress can be destructive. But are there positive sides to stress as well?

Yes, but let's define what stress is first. Stress is a physiological response to any change, whether good or bad, that alerts the adaptive fight-or-flight response in the brain and the body. Good stress, also called *eustress,* gives us energy and motivates us to strive and produce. We see eustress in elite athletes, creative artists, and all kinds of high achievers. Anyone who's clinched an important deal or had a good performance review, for example, enjoys the benefits of eustress, such as clear thinking, focus, and creative insight.

But when most people talk about stress, they are referring to the bad kind. At work, negative stressors are usually the perceived actions of customers, clients, bosses, colleagues, and employees, combined with demanding deadlines. At the Mind/Body Medical Institute, we also encounter executives who worry incessantly about . . . the impact of China on their companies' markets, the state of the economy, the world oil supply, and so on. Additionally, people bring to work the stress aroused by dealing with family problems, taxes, and traffic jams, as well as anxieties stemming from a continuous diet of bad news that upsets them and makes them feel helpless—hurricanes, politics, child abductions, wars, terrorist attacks, environmental devastation, you name it.

Many companies offer various kinds of stress-reduction programs, from on-site yoga classes and massage to fancy gyms to workshops. What's wrong with these?

It's critical that companies do something to address the rampant negative effects of workplace stress if they want to compete effectively, but often the kinds of programs they institute are stopgaps. HR may bring in a lecturer once or twice a year or set up tai chi sessions and urge everyone to go, but few people show up because they feel they can't take the time to eat their lunch, much less spend an hour doing something perceived as both unrelated to work and relaxing to boot. Unless the leadership and culture explicitly encourage people to join in, employees will continue to feel guilty or worry that they'll be seen as slackers if they go.

This state of affairs is inexcusable if you look at the billions lost to absenteeism, turnover, disability, insurance costs, workplace accidents, violence, workers' compensation, and lawsuits, not to mention the expense of replacing valuable employees lost to stress-related problems. Fortunately, each of us holds the key for managing stress, and leaders who learn to do this and help their employees to do likewise can tap into enormous productivity and potential while mitigating these costs.

What is the science behind your research, and what does it reveal?

First, let me say that we at the Mind/Body Medical Institute didn't discover anything new. The American philosopher William James identified the breakout principle in his *Varieties of Religious Experience* in 1902. What we set about to do was explore the science behind what James had identified.

Over the past [several decades], our teams have collected data on thousands of subjects from population studies, physiologic measurements, brain imaging, molecular biology, biochemistry, and other approaches to measuring bodily reactions to stress. From these we identified the relaxation response and could see how powerful it was. It is a physical state of deep rest that counteracts the harmful effects of the fight-or-flight response, such as increased heart rate, blood pressure, and muscle tension.

Neurologically, what happens is this: When we encounter a stressor at work—a difficult employee, a tough negotiation, a tight deadline, or worse—we can deal with it for a little while before the negative effects set in. But if we are exposed for excessively long periods to the fight-or-flight response, the pressure on us will become too great, and our system will be flooded with the hormones epinephrine, norepinephrine, and cortisol. These cause blood pressure to rise and the heart rate and brain activity to increase, effects that are very deleterious over time. But our . . . findings indicate that by completely letting go of a problem at that point by applying certain triggers, the brain actually rearranges itself so that the hemispheres communicate better. Then the brain is better able to solve the problem.

The best way to understand this mechanism is to go back [about] 100 years to the work of two Harvard researchers, Robert Yerkes and John Dodson. In 1908, these two demonstrated that efficiency increases when stress increases, but only up to a point; after that, performance falls off dramatically (see figure 1-1). We found

FIGURE 1-1

The Yerkes-Dodson curve

Stress is an essential response in highly competitive environments. Before a race, before an exam, before an important meeting, your heart rate goes up and so does your blood pressure. You become more focused, alert, and efficient. But past a certain level, stress compromises your performance, efficiency, and eventually your health. Two Harvard researchers, Robert M. Yerkes and John D. Dodson, first calibrated the relationship between stress and performance in 1908, which has been dubbed the Yerkes-Dodson law.

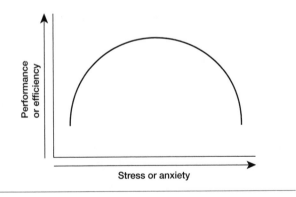

that by taking the stress level up to the top of the bell curve and then effectively pulling the rug out from under it by turning to a quieting, rejuvenating activity, subjects could evoke the relaxation response, which effectively counteracts the negative effects of the stress hormones. Molecular studies have shown that the calming response releases little "puffs" of nitric oxide, which has been linked to the production of such neurotransmitters as endorphins and dopamine. These chemicals enhance general feelings of well-being. As the brain quiets down, another phenomenon that we call *calm commotion*—or a focused increase in activity—takes place in the areas of the brain associated with attention, space-time concepts, and decision making.

In eliciting the relaxation response, individuals experience a sudden creative insight, in which the solution to the problem becomes apparent. This is a momentary phenomenon. Thereafter, the subjects enter a state of sustained improved performance, which we call the *new-normal* state, because the breakthrough effect can be remembered indefinitely.

We find this to be an intriguing phenomenon. By bringing the brain to the height of activity and then suddenly moving it into a passive, relaxed state, it's possible to stimulate much higher neurological performance than would otherwise be the case. Over time, subjects who learn to do this as a matter of course perform at consistently higher levels. The effect is particularly noticeable in athletes and creative artists, but we have also seen it among the businesspeople we work with.

So how can we actually go about tapping into the breakout principle?

A breakout sequence occurs in four steps. The first step is to struggle mightily with a thorny problem. For a businessperson, this may be concentrated problem analysis or fact gathering; it can also simply be thinking intently about a stressful situation at work—a tough employee, a performance conundrum, a budgetary difficulty. The key is to put a significant amount of preliminary hard work into the matter. Basically, you want to lean into the problem to get to the top of the Yerkes-Dodson curve.

You can tell when you have neared the top of the curve when you stop feeling productive and start feeling stressed. You may have unpleasant feelings such as anxiety, fearfulness, anger, or boredom, or you may feel like procrastinating. You may even have physical symptoms such as a headache, a knot in the stomach, or sweaty palms. At this point, it's time to move to step two.

Step two involves walking away from the problem and doing something utterly different that produces the relaxation response. There are many ways to do this. A 10-minute relaxation-response exercise, in which you calm your mind and focus on your out-breath while disregarding the thoughts you've been having, works extremely well. Some people go jogging or pet a furry animal; others look at paintings they love. Some relax in a sauna or take a hot shower. Still others "sleep on it" by taking a nap or getting a good night's rest, having a meal with friends, or listening to their favorite calming music.

One male executive I know relaxes by doing needlepoint. All of these things bring about the mental rearrangement that is the foundation for new insights, solutions, and creativity. The key is to stop analyzing, surrender control, and completely detach yourself from the stress-producing thoughts. When you allow your brain to quiet down, your body releases the puffs of nitric oxide that make you feel better and make you more productive.

One executive we observed was worried about a big presentation she had to make before some top-level managers. She worked and worked on it, but the harder she worked, the more befuddled she became and the more anxiety took over. Fortunately, she had learned to evoke her relaxation response by visiting the art museum near her office. So she did. After a while, she felt a sense of total release as she stood there looking at her favorite pictures. At that point, she suddenly had the insight that she was trying to cover too many topics at once and needed to pare down the presentation to a single, over-riding concept she could illustrate with solid examples. She felt inspired and confident that she had the answer. She went back to the office, redid the presentation, and, feeling relaxed and happy, went home for the day.

This third step—gaining a sudden insight—is the actual breakout. Breakouts are also often referred to as *peak experiences, flow,* or *being in the zone.* Elite athletes reach this state when they train hard and then let go and allow the muscle memory to take over. They become completely immersed in what they're doing, which feels automatic, smooth, and effortless. In all cases, a breakout is experienced as a sense of well-being and relaxation that brings with it an unexpected insight or a higher level of performance. And it's all the result of a simple biological mechanism that we can tap into at will.

The final step is the return to the new-normal state, in which the sense of self-confidence continues. The manager who reorganized her presentation, for example, came in the next morning knowing all would be well. The meeting did go well, and she received accolades for her work from her bosses and colleagues.

Does a breakout occur all the time or just occasionally? What percentage of people, according to your research, experience breakouts in this way?

We don't yet have hard data on this, but anecdotally I can tell you that when you compare groups of people who have been trained to evoke the relaxation response to groups who lack such training, the former experience breakouts much more frequently. About 25% of people trained in this process, and sometimes many more, can reliably reach the breakout stage.

It sometimes takes a serious illness caused or exacerbated by stress for people to have their "aha" moments. One well-known CEO we worked with spent years putting in more than 60 hours a week at his intensely stressful job. He came to us after he had been diagnosed with a silent heart attack. His world had completely turned upside down. He took a leave of absence from work to focus on healing, to ask himself why he was on the planet, and to spend time with his family. We trained him to use the relaxation response and the breakout principle. He recovered and came back to work far more resilient and productive than he was before.

Can teams or groups do this together or somehow feed off one another?

Certainly. The benefits of mind/body management are by no means limited to individuals. Those who become skilled in these techniques can also expect to have an exponential impact in groups or teams; they can work together to solve organizational problems as part of what we might call a *mind/body orchestra*.

Let me give you an example of how this works. A few years ago, three software executives with whom we had worked spent two days trying to cajole venture capitalists in Singapore to fund several projects having to do with a new kind of encryption technology. They had all thought long and hard about the problems with encryption, both at their home office in the States and in their preparations for the Singapore presentation. This produced significant levels of stress hormones.

After the meetings finally ended, the three of them took a cab to the airport. The drive was long, and they all felt they could finally let their hair down and relax. Through no planning on anyone's part, the environment in the taxi produced the required break from prior thinking patterns and emotions. The sense of relief, the release from days of high stress, the feeling of camaraderie, and the mentally lulling ride in the dark taxi clearly triggered the relaxation response. That put them all in a neurological position to focus and think clearly about encryption.

The inventor of the technology was the most creative thinker of the three, the one who could best integrate his left- and right-brain functions. He tossed out a thought that had just come to him for a revolutionary product. The others, who were more linear and practical in their thinking style, got excited and chimed in with all kinds of questions and ideas for marketing and selling it. By the end of the cab ride, the trio had fashioned an entirely new encryption product—without taking a single note as the final idea emerged in their minds. They filed a provisional patent three weeks afterward and their final patent application one year later. They are now selling a version of the product as part of a multimillion-dollar enterprise.

―――――――――

Bronwyn Fryer was a senior editor at *Harvard Business Review.*

Chapter 2
Overloaded Circuits

Why Smart People Underperform

by Edward M. Hallowell

IDEA IN BRIEF

Frenzied executives who fidget through meetings, miss appointments, and jab at the elevator's "door close" button aren't crazy—just crazed. They're suffering from a newly recognized neurological phenomenon called **attention deficit trait (ADT).** Marked by distractibility, inner frenzy, and impatience, ADT prevents managers from clarifying priorities, making smart decisions, and managing their time. This insidious condition turns

Reprinted from *Harvard Business Review*, January 2005 (product #R0501E)

otherwise talented performers into harried underachievers. And it's reaching epidemic proportions.

ADT isn't an illness or character defect. It's our brains' natural response to exploding demands on our time and attention. As data increasingly floods our brains, we lose our ability to solve problems and handle the unknown. Creativity shrivels; mistakes multiply. Some sufferers eventually melt down.

How to control ADT's ravaging impact on performance? *Foster positive emotions* by connecting face-to-face with people you like throughout the day. *Take physical care of your brain* by getting enough sleep, eating healthfully, and exercising regularly. *Organize for ADT*, designating part of each day for thinking and planning, and setting up your office to foster mental functioning (for example, keeping part of your desk clear at all times).

These strategies may seem like no-brainers. But they'll help you vanquish the ADT demon before it can strike.

IDEA IN PRACTICE

How You Can Combat ADT

Promote positive emotions

Negative emotions—especially fear—can hamper productive brain functioning. To promote positive feelings, especially during highly stressful times, interact directly with someone you like at least every four to six hours. In environments where people are in physical contact with people they trust, brain functioning hums. By connecting comfortably with colleagues, you'll help your brain's "executive" center (responsible for decision making, planning, and information prioritizing) perform at its best.

Take physical care of your brain

Ample sleep, a good diet, and exercise are critical for staving off ADT. You're getting enough sleep if you can awake without an alarm clock. You're eating well if you're avoiding sugar and white flour and consuming more fruits, whole grains, vegetables, and protein instead. You're exercising enough if you're taking a brisk walk or going up and down a flight of stairs a few times a day.

Organize for ADT

Instead of getting sucked into the vortices of e-mail or voice mail first thing in the morning, attend to a critical task. With paperwork, apply the OHIO ("Only handle it once") rule: Whenever you touch a document, act on it, file it, or throw it away. Do crucial work during times of the day when you perform at your best. Use whatever small strategies help you function well mentally—whether it's listening to music or walking around while working, or doodling during meetings. And before you leave for the day, list three to five priority items you'll need to address tomorrow.

What Your Company Can Do

In firms that ignore ADT symptoms, employees underachieve, create clutter, and cut corners. Careless mistakes, illness, and turnover increase, as people squander their brain power. To counteract ADT and harness employees' brainpower, invest in amenities that foster a positive, productive atmosphere.

> *Example:* Major software company SAS Institute creates a warm, connected, and relaxed work environment by offering employees perks such as a seven-hour workday that ends at 5:00; large on-site gym and day care facility; and a cafeteria that provides baby seats and high chairs so parents can eat lunch with their children. The payoff? Employees return the favors with high productivity. And SAS's turnover never exceeds 5%—saving the company millions on recruiting, training, and severance.

David drums his fingers on his desk as he scans the e-mail on his computer screen. At the same time, he's talking on the phone to an executive halfway around the world. His knee bounces up and down like a jackhammer. He intermittently bites his lip and reaches for his constant companion, the coffee cup. He's so deeply involved in multitasking that he has forgotten the appointment his Outlook calendar reminded him of 15 minutes ago.

Jane, a senior vice president, and Mike, her CEO, have adjoining offices so they can communicate quickly, yet communication never seems to happen. "Whenever I go into Mike's office, his phone lights up, my cell phone goes off, someone knocks on the door, he suddenly turns to his screen and writes an e-mail, or he tells me about a new issue he wants me to address," Jane complains.

"We're working flat out just to stay afloat, and we're not getting anything important accomplished. It's driving me crazy."

David, Jane, and Mike aren't crazy, but they're certainly crazed. Their experience is becoming the norm for overworked managers who suffer—like many of your colleagues, and possibly like you—from a very real but unrecognized neurological phenomenon that I call attention deficit trait, or ADT. Caused by brain overload, ADT is now epidemic in organizations. The core symptoms are distractibility, inner frenzy, and impatience. People with ADT have difficulty staying organized, setting priorities, and managing time. These symptoms can undermine the work of an otherwise gifted executive. If David, Jane, Mike, and the millions like them understood themselves in neurological terms, they could actively manage their lives instead of reacting to problems as they happen.

As a psychiatrist who has diagnosed and treated thousands of people over the past 25 years for a medical condition called attention deficit disorder, or ADD (now known clinically as attention-deficit/hyperactivity disorder), I have observed firsthand how a rapidly growing segment of the adult population is developing this new, related condition. The number of people with ADT coming into my clinical practice has mushroomed by a factor of 10 in the past decade. Unfortunately, most of the remedies for chronic overload proposed by time-management consultants and executive coaches do not address the underlying causes of ADT.

Unlike ADD, a neurological disorder that has a genetic component and can be aggravated by environmental and physical factors, ADT springs entirely from the environment. Like the traffic jam, ADT is an artifact of modern life. It is brought on by the demands on our time and attention that have exploded over the past two decades. As our minds fill with noise—feckless synaptic events signifying nothing—the brain gradually loses its capacity to attend fully and thoroughly to anything.

The symptoms of ADT come upon a person gradually. The sufferer doesn't experience a single crisis but rather a series of minor emergencies while he or she tries harder and harder to keep up. Shouldering a responsibility to "suck it up" and not complain as the workload increases, executives with ADT do whatever they can to handle a load they simply cannot manage as well as they'd like. The ADT sufferer therefore feels a constant low level of panic and guilt. Facing a tidal wave of tasks, the executive becomes increasingly hurried, curt, peremptory, and unfocused, while pretending that everything is fine.

To control ADT, we first have to recognize it. And control it we must, if we as individuals and organizational leaders are to be effective. In the following pages, I'll offer an analysis of the origins of ADT and provide some suggestions that may help you manage it.

Attention Deficit Cousins

To understand the nature and treatment of ADT, it's useful to know something of its cousin, ADD.

Usually seen as a learning disability in children, ADD also afflicts about 5% of the adult population. Researchers using MRI scans have found that people with ADD suffer a slightly diminished volume in four specific brain regions that have various functions such as modulating emotion (especially anger and frustration) and assisting in learning. One of the regions, made up of the frontal and prefrontal lobes, generates thoughts, makes decisions, sets priorities, and organizes activities. While the medications used to treat ADD don't change the anatomy of the brain, they alter brain chemistry, which in turn improves function in each of the four regions and so dramatically bolsters the performance of ADD sufferers.

ADD confers both disadvantages and advantages. The negative characteristics include a tendency to procrastinate and miss deadlines. People with ADD struggle with disorganization and tardiness; they can be forgetful and drift away mentally in the middle of a conversation or while reading. Their performance can be inconsistent: brilliant one moment and unsatisfactory the next. ADD sufferers also tend to demonstrate impatience and lose focus unless, oddly enough, they are under stress or handling multiple inputs. (This is because stress leads to the production of adrenaline, which is chemically similar to the medications we use to treat ADD.) Finally, people with ADD sometimes also self-medicate with excessive alcohol or other substances.

On the positive side, those with ADD usually possess rare talents and gifts. Those gifts often go unnoticed or undeveloped, however, because of the problems caused by the condition's negative symptoms. ADD sufferers can be remarkably creative and original. They are unusually persistent under certain circumstances and often possess an entrepreneurial flair. They display ingenuity and encourage that trait in others. They tend to improvise well under pressure. Because they have the ability to field multiple inputs simultaneously, they can be strong leaders during times of change. They also tend to rebound quickly after setbacks and bring fresh energy to the company every day.

Executives with ADD typically achieve inconsistent results. Sometimes they fail miserably because they're disorganized and make mistakes. At other times, they perform brilliantly, offering original ideas and strategies that lead to performance at the highest level.

David Neeleman, the CEO of JetBlue Airways, has ADD. School was torture; unable to focus, he hated to study and procrastinated endlessly. "I felt like I should be out doing things, moving things along, but here I was, stuck studying statistics, which I knew had no application to my life," Neeleman told me. "I knew I had to have an education, but at the first opportunity to start a business, I just blew out of college." He climbed quickly in the corporate world, making use of his strengths—original thinking, high energy, an ability to draw out the best in people—and getting help with organization and time management.

Like most people with ADD, Neeleman could sometimes offend with his blunt words, but his ideas were good enough to change the airline industry. For example, he invented the electronic ticket. "When I proposed that idea, people laughed at me, saying no one would go to the airport without a paper ticket," he says. "Now everyone does, and it has saved the industry millions of dollars." It seems fitting that someone with ADD would invent a way around having to remember to bring a paper ticket.

Neeleman believes ADD is one of the keys to his success. Far from regretting having it, he celebrates it. But he understands that he must manage his ADD carefully.

Attention deficit trait is characterized by ADD's negative symptoms. Rather than being rooted in genetics, however, ADT is purely a response to the hyperkinetic environment in which we live. Indeed, modern culture all but requires many of us to develop ADT. Never in history has the human brain been asked to track so many data points. Everywhere, people rely on their cell phones, e-mail, and digital assistants in the race to gather and transmit data, plans, and ideas faster and faster. One could argue that the chief value of the modern era is speed, which the novelist Milan Kundera described as "the form of ecstasy that technology has bestowed upon modern man." Addicted to speed, we demand it even when we can't possibly go faster. James Gleick wryly noted in *Faster: The Acceleration of Just About Everything* that the "close door" button in elevators is often the one with the paint worn off. As the human brain struggles to keep up, it falters and then falls into the world of ADT.

This Is Your Brain

While brain scans cannot display anatomical differences between people with "normal" brains and people suffering from ADT, studies have shown that as the human brain is asked to process dizzying amounts of data, its ability to solve problems flexibly and creatively declines and the number of mistakes increases. To find out why, let's go on a brief neurological journey.

Blessed with the largest cortex in all of nature, own-
ers of this trillion-celled organ today put singular pressure on the frontal and prefrontal lobes, which I'll refer
to in this article as simply the frontal lobes. This region
governs what is called, aptly enough, executive functioning (EF). EF guides decision making and planning; the
organization and prioritization of information and ideas;
time management; and various other sophisticated,
uniquely human, managerial tasks. As long as our frontal
lobes remain in charge, everything is fine.

Beneath the frontal lobes lie the parts of the brain de-
voted to survival. These deep centers govern basic functions like sleep, hunger, sexual desire, breathing, and
heart rate, as well as crudely positive and negative emotions. When you are doing well and operating at peak
level, the deep centers send up messages of excitement,
satisfaction, and joy. They pump up your motivation, help
you maintain attention, and don't interfere with working
memory, the number of data points you can keep track
of at once. But when you are confronted with the sixth
decision after the fifth interruption in the midst of a
search for the ninth missing piece of information on the
day that the third deal has collapsed and the 12th impossible request has blipped unbidden across your computer
screen, your brain begins to panic, reacting just as if that
sixth decision were a bloodthirsty, man-eating tiger.

As a specialist in learning disabilities, I have found
that the most dangerous disability is not any formally di-
agnosable condition like dyslexia or ADD. It is fear. Fear
shifts us into survival mode and thus prevents fluid learning and nuanced understanding. Certainly, if a real tiger

is about to attack you, survival is the mode you want to be in. But if you're trying to deal intelligently with a subtle task, survival mode is highly unpleasant and counter-productive.

When the frontal lobes approach capacity and we begin to fear that we can't keep up, the relationship between the higher and lower regions of the brain takes an ominous turn. Thousands of years of evolution have taught the higher brain not to ignore the lower brain's distress signals. In survival mode, the deep areas of the brain assume control and begin to direct the higher regions. As a result, the whole brain gets caught in a neurological catch-22. The deep regions interpret the messages of overload they receive from the frontal lobes in the same way they interpret everything: primitively. They furiously fire signals of fear, anxiety, impatience, irritability, anger, or panic. These alarm signals shanghai the attention of the frontal lobes, forcing them to forfeit much of their power. Because survival signals are irresistible, the frontal lobes get stuck sending messages back to the deep centers saying, "Message received. Trying to work on it but without success." These messages further perturb the deep centers, which send even more powerful messages of distress back up to the frontal lobes.

Meanwhile, in response to what's going on in the brain, the rest of the body—particularly the endocrine, respiratory, cardiovascular, musculoskeletal, and peripheral nervous systems—has shifted into crisis mode and changed its baseline physiology from peace and quiet to red alert. The brain and body are locked in a reverberating circuit while the frontal lobes lose their sophistication, as if vinegar were added to wine. In this state, EF reverts to simpleminded black-and-white thinking; perspective and shades of gray disappear. Intelligence dims. In a futile attempt to do more than is possible, the brain paradoxically reduces its ability to think clearly.

This neurological event occurs when a manager is desperately trying to deal with more input than he possibly can. In survival mode, the manager makes impulsive judgments, angrily rushing to bring closure to whatever matter is at hand. He feels compelled to get the problem under control immediately, to extinguish the perceived danger lest it destroy him. He is robbed of his flexibility, his sense of humor, his ability to deal with the unknown. He forgets the big picture and the goals and values he stands for. He loses his creativity and his ability to change plans. He desperately wants to kill the metaphorical tiger. At these moments he is prone to melting down, to throwing a tantrum, to blaming others, and to sabotaging himself. Or he may go in the opposite direction, falling into denial and total avoidance of the problems attacking him, only to be devoured. This is ADT at its worst.

Though ADT does not always reach such extreme proportions, it does wreak havoc among harried workers. Because no two brains are alike, some people deal with the condition better than others. Regardless of how well executives appear to function, however, no one has total control over his or her executive functioning.

Managing ADT

Unfortunately, top management has so far viewed the symptoms of ADT through the distorting lens of morality or character. Employees who seem unable to keep up the pace are seen as deficient or weak. Consider the case of an executive who came to see me when he was completely overloaded. I suggested he talk the situation over with his superior and ask for help. When my client did so, he was told that if he couldn't handle the work, he ought to think about resigning. Even though his performance assessments were stellar and he'd earned praise for being one of the most creative people in the organization, he was allowed to leave. Because the firm sought to preserve the myth that no straw would ever break its people's backs, it could not tolerate the manager's stating that his back was breaking. After he went out on his own, he flourished.

How can we control the rampaging effects of ADT, both in ourselves and in our organizations? While ADD often requires medication, the treatment of ADT certainly does not. ADT can be controlled only by creatively engineering one's environment and one's emotional and physical health. I have found that the following preventive measures go a long way toward helping executives control their symptoms of ADT.

Promote positive emotions

The most important step in controlling ADT is not to buy a superturbocharged BlackBerry and fill it up with to-dos but rather to create an environment in which the brain can function at its best. This means building a positive, fear-free emotional atmosphere, because emotion is the on/off switch for executive functioning.

There are neurological reasons why ADT occurs less in environments where people are in physical contact and where they trust and respect one another. When you comfortably connect with a colleague, even if you are dealing with an overwhelming problem, the deep centers of the brain send messages through the pleasure center to the area that assigns resources to the frontal lobes. Even when you're under extreme stress, this sense of human connection causes executive functioning to hum.

By contrast, people who work in physical isolation are more likely to suffer from ADT, for the more isolated we are, the more stressed we become. I witnessed a dramatic example of the danger of a disconnected environment and the healing power of a connected one when I consulted for one of the world's foremost university chemistry departments. In the department's formerly hard-driven culture, ADT was rampant, exacerbated by an ethic that forbade anyone to ask for help or even state that anything was wrong. People did not trust one another; they worked on projects alone, which led to more mistrust. Most people were in emotional pain, but implicit in the department's culture was the notion that great pain led to great gain.

In the late 1990s, one of the department's most gifted graduate students killed himself. His suicide note explicitly blamed the university for pushing him past his limit. The department's culture was literally lethal.

Instead of trying to sweep the tragedy under the rug, the chair of the department and his successor acted boldly and creatively. They immediately changed the structure of the supervisory system so that each graduate student and postdoc was assigned three supervisors, rather than a single one with a death grip on the trainee's career. The department set up informal biweekly buffets that allowed people to connect. (Even the most reclusive chemist came out of hiding for food, one of life's great connectors.) The department heads went as far as changing the architecture of the department's main building, taking down walls and adding common areas and an espresso bar complete with a grand piano. They provided lectures and written information to all students about the danger signs of mental wear and tear and offered confidential procedures for students who needed help. These steps, along with regular meetings that included senior faculty and university administrators, led to a more humane, productive culture in which the students and faculty felt fully engaged. The department's performance remained first-rate, and creative research blossomed.

The bottom line is this: Fostering connections and reducing fear promote brainpower. When you make time at least every four to six hours for a "human moment," a face-to-face exchange with a person you like, you are giving your brain what it needs.

Take physical care of your brain

Sleep, a good diet, and exercise are critical for staving off ADT. Though this sounds like a no-brainer, too many of us abuse our brains by neglecting obvious principles of care.

You may try to cope with ADT by sleeping less, in the vain hope that you can get more done. This is the opposite of what you need to do, for ADT sets in when you don't get enough sleep. There is ample documentation to suggest that sleep deprivation engenders a host of problems, from impaired decision making and reduced creativity to reckless behavior and paranoia. We vary in how much sleep we require; a good rule of thumb is that you're getting enough sleep if you can wake up without an alarm clock.

Diet also plays a crucial role in brain health. Many hardworking people habitually inhale carbohydrates, which cause blood glucose levels to yo-yo. This leads to a vicious cycle: Rapid fluctuations in insulin levels further increase the craving for carbohydrates. The brain, which relies on glucose for energy, is left either glutted or gasping, neither of which makes for optimal cognitive functioning.

The brain does much better if the blood glucose level can be held relatively stable. To do this, avoid simple carbohydrates containing sugar and white flour (pastries, white bread, and pasta, for example). Rely on the complex carbohydrates found in fruits, whole grains, and vegetables. Protein is important: Instead of starting your day with coffee and a Danish, try tea and an egg or a piece of smoked salmon on wheat toast. Take a multivitamin every day as well as supplementary omega-3 fatty acids, an excellent source of which is fish oil. The omega-3s and the E and B complex contained in multivitamins promote healthy brain function and may even stave off Alzheimer's disease and inflammatory ills (which can be the starting point for major killers like heart disease, stroke, diabetes, and cancer). Moderate your intake of alcohol, too, because too much kills brain cells and accelerates the development of memory loss and even dementia. As you change your diet to promote optimal brain function and good general health, your body will also shed excess pounds.

If you think you can't afford the time to exercise, think again. Sitting at a desk for hours on end decreases mental acuity, not only because of reduced blood flow to the brain but for other biochemical reasons as well. Physical exercise induces the body to produce an array of chemicals that the brain loves, including endorphins, serotonin, dopamine, epinephrine, and norepinephrine, as well as two recently discovered compounds, brain-derived neurotrophic factor (BDNF) and nerve growth factor (NGF). Both BDNF and NGF promote cell health and development in the brain, stave off the ravages of aging and stress, and keep the brain in tip-top condition. Nothing stimulates the production of BDNF and NGF as robustly as physical exercise, which explains why those who exercise regularly talk about the letdown and sluggishness they experience if they miss their exercise for a few days. You will more than compensate for the time you invest on the treadmill with improved productivity and efficiency. To fend off the symptoms of ADT while you're at work, get up from your desk and go up and down a flight of stairs a few times or walk briskly down a hallway. These quick, simple efforts will push your brain's reset button.

Organize for ADT

It's important to develop tactics for getting organized, but not in the sense of empty New Year's resolutions. Rather, your goal is to order your work in a way that suits you, so that disorganization does not keep you from reaching your goals.

First, devise strategies to help your frontal lobes stay in control. These might include breaking down large tasks into smaller ones and keeping a section of your work space or desk clear at all times. (You do not need to have a neat office, just a neat section of your office.) Similarly, you might try keeping a portion of your day free of appointments, e-mail, and other distractions so that you have time to think and plan. Because e-mail is a wonderful way to procrastinate and set yourself up for ADT at the same time, you might consider holding specific "e-mail hours," since it isn't necessary to reply to every e-mail right away.

When you start your day, don't allow yourself to get sucked into vortices of e-mail or voice mail or into attending to minor tasks that eat up your time but don't pack a punch. Attend to a critical task instead. Before you leave for the day, make a list of no more than five priority items that will require your attention tomorrow. Short lists force you to prioritize and complete your tasks. Additionally, keep torrents of documents at bay. One of my patients, an executive with ADD, uses the OHIO rule: Only handle it once. If he touches a document, he acts on it, files it, or throws it away. "I don't put it in a pile," he says. "Piles are like weeds. If you let them grow, they take over everything."

Pay attention to the times of day when you feel that you perform at your best; do your most important work then and save the rote work for other times. Set up your office in a way that helps mental functioning. If you focus better with music, have music (if need be, use earphones). If you think best on your feet, work standing up or walk around frequently. If doodling or drumming your fingers helps, figure out a way to do so without bothering anyone, or get a fidget toy to bring to meetings. These small strategies sound mundane, but they address the ADT devil that resides in distracting details.

Protect your frontal lobes

To stay out of survival mode and keep your lower brain from usurping control, slow down. Take the time you need to comprehend what is going on, to listen, to ask questions, and to digest what's been said so that you don't get confused and send your brain into panic. Empower an assistant to ride herd on you; insist that he or she tell you to stop e-mailing, get off the telephone, or leave the office.

If you do begin to feel overwhelmed, try the following mind-clearing tricks. Do an easy rote task, such as resetting the calendar on your watch or writing a memo on a neutral topic. If you feel anxious about beginning a project, pull out a sheet of paper or fire up your word processor and write a paragraph about something unrelated to the project (a description of your house, your car, your shoes—anything you know well). You can also tackle the easiest part of the task; for example, write just the title of a memo about it. Open a dictionary and read a few definitions, or spend five minutes doing a crossword puzzle. Each of these little tasks quiets your lower brain by tricking it into shutting off alarmist messages and puts your frontal lobes back in full control.

Finally, be ready for the next attack of ADT by posting the sidebar "Control Your ADT" near your desk where

In General

- Get adequate sleep.

- Watch what you eat. Avoid simple, sugary carbohydrates, moderate your intake of alcohol, add protein, stick to complex carbohydrates (vegetables, whole grains, fruit).

- Exercise at least 30 minutes at least every other day.

- Take a daily multivitamin and an omega-3 fatty acid supplement.

At Work

- Do all you can to create a trusting, connected work environment.

- Have a friendly, face-to-face talk with a person you like every four to six hours.

- Break large tasks into smaller ones.

- Keep a section of your work space or desk clear at all times.

- Each day, reserve some "think time" that's free from appointments, e-mail, and phone calls.

- Set aside e-mail until you've completed at least one or two more important tasks.

- Before you leave work each day, create a short list of three to five items you will attend to the next day.

- Try to act on, file, or toss every document you touch.

- Don't let papers accumulate.

- Pay attention to the times of day when you feel that you are at your best; do your most important work then, and save the rote work for other times.

- Do whatever you need to do to work in a more focused way: Add background music, walk around, and so on.

- Ask a colleague or an assistant to help you stop talking on the telephone, e-mailing, or working too late.

When You Feel Overwhelmed

- Slow down.

- Do an easy rote task: Reset your watch, write a note about a neutral topic (such as a description of your house), read a few dictionary definitions, do a short crossword puzzle.

- Move around: Go up and down a flight of stairs or walk briskly.

- Ask for help, delegate a task, or brainstorm with a colleague. In short, do not worry alone.

you can see it. Knowing that you are prepared diminishes the likelihood of an attack, because you're not susceptible to panic.

What Leaders Can Do

All too often, companies induce and exacerbate ADT in their employees by demanding fast thinking rather than deep thinking. Firms also ask employees to work on multiple overlapping projects and initiatives, resulting in second-rate thinking. Worse, companies that ask their employees to do too much at once tend to reward those who say yes to overload while punishing those who choose to focus and say no.

Moreover, organizations make the mistake of forcing their employees to do more and more with less and less by eliminating support staff. Such companies end up losing money in the long run, for the more time a manager has to spend being his own administrative assistant and the less he is able to delegate, the less effective he will be in doing the important work of moving the organization forward. Additionally, firms that ignore the symptoms of ADT in their employees suffer its ill effects: Employees underachieve, create clutter, cut corners, make careless mistakes, and squander their brainpower. As demands continue to increase, a toxic, high-pressure environment leads to high rates of employee illness and turnover.

To counteract ADT and harness employee brainpower, firms should invest in amenities that contribute to a positive atmosphere. One company that has done an excellent job in this regard is SAS Institute, a major software company in North Carolina. The company famously offers its employees a long list of perks: a 36,000-square-foot, on-site gym; a seven-hour workday that ends at 5 PM; the largest on-site day care facility in North Carolina; a cafeteria that provides baby seats and high chairs so parents can eat lunch with their children; unlimited sick days; and much more. The atmosphere at SAS is warm, connected, and relaxed. The effect on the bottom line is profoundly positive; turnover is never higher than 5%. The company saves the millions other software companies spend on recruiting, training, and severance (estimated to be at least 1.5 times salary in the software industry). Employees return the favors with high productivity. The forces of ADT that shred other organizations never gain momentum at SAS.

Leaders can also help prevent ADT by matching employees' skills to tasks. When managers assign goals that stretch people too far or ask workers to focus on what they're not good at rather than what they do well, stress rises. By contrast, managers who understand the dangers of ADT can find ways of keeping themselves and their organizations on track. JetBlue's David Neeleman, for example, has shamelessly and publicly identified what he is not good at and found ways to deal with his shortcomings, either by delegating or by empowering his assistant to direct him. Neeleman also models this behavior for everyone else in the organization. His openness about the challenges of his ADD gives others permission to speak about their own attention deficit difficulties and to garner the support they need. He also encourages his managers to match people with tasks that fit their cognitive and emotional styles, knowing that no one style is best. Neeleman believes that helping people work to their strengths is not just a mark of sophisticated management; it's also an excellent way to boost worker productivity and morale.

ADT is a very real threat to all of us. If we do not manage it, it manages us. But an understanding of ADT and its ravages allows us to apply practical methods to improve our work and our lives. In the end, the most critical step an enlightened leader can take to address the problem of ADT is to name it. Bringing ADT out of the closet and describing its symptoms removes the stigma and eliminates the moral condemnation companies have for so long mistakenly leveled at overburdened employees. By giving people permission to ask for help and remaining vigilant for signs of stress, organizations will go a long way toward fostering more productive, well-balanced, and intelligent work environments.

Edward M. "Ned" Hallowell, MD, is a psychiatrist and the founder of the Hallowell Center for Cognitive and Emotional Health in Sudbury, Massachusetts. He is the author of *Shine: Using Brain Science to Get the Best from Your People* (Harvard Business Review Press, 2011).

Section 2
Renewing Your Energy

Chapter 3
Manage Your Energy, Not Your Time

by Tony Schwartz and Catherine McCarthy

A summary of the full-length HBR article by **Tony Schwartz** *and* **Catherine McCarthy**, *highlighting key ideas.*

IDEA IN BRIEF

Is your job demanding more from you than ever before? Do you feel as if you're working additional hours but rarely getting ahead? Is your mobile device leashing

Reprinted from *Harvard Business Review*, October 2007 (product #R0710B)

you to your job 24/7? Do you feel exhausted, disengaged, sick?

Spending longer days at the office and putting in extra hours at home doesn't work because your time is a limited resource. But your personal energy is renewable. By fostering deceptively simple *rituals* that will help you regularly replenish your energy, you can strengthen your physical, emotional, mental, and spiritual resilience. These rituals include taking brief breaks at specific intervals, expressing appreciation to others, reducing interruptions, and spending more time on the activities you do best and enjoy most.

IDEA IN PRACTICE

Try these practices to renew the four dimensions of your personal energy:

Physical Energy

- Enhance your sleep by setting an earlier bedtime and reducing alcohol use.

- Reduce stress by engaging in cardiovascular activity at least three times a week and strength training at least once a week.

- Eat small meals and light snacks every three hours.

- Learn to notice signs of imminent flagging energy, including restlessness, yawning, hunger, and difficulty concentrating.

- Take brief but regular breaks away from your desk at 90- to 120-minute intervals throughout the day.

Emotional Energy

- Defuse negative emotions—irritability, impatience, anxiety, insecurity—through deep abdominal breathing.

- Fuel positive emotions in yourself and others by regularly expressing appreciation to people in detailed, specific terms through notes, e-mails, calls, or conversations.

- Look at upsetting situations through new lenses. Adopt a *reverse lens* to ask, "What would the other person in this conflict say, and how might he be right?" Use a *long lens* to ask, "How will I likely view this situation in six months?" Employ a *wide lens* to ask, "How can I grow and learn from this situation?"

Mental Energy

- Reduce interruptions by performing high-concentration tasks away from phones and e-mail.

- Respond to voice mails and e-mails at designated times during the day.

- Select the most important challenge for the next day the night before. Then make that challenge your first priority when you arrive at work in the morning.

Spiritual Energy

- Identify your "sweet spot" activities—those that give you feelings of effectiveness, effortless absorption, and fulfillment. Find ways to do more of these. One executive who hated doing sales reports delegated them to someone who loved that activity.

- Allocate time and energy to what you consider most important. For example, spend the last 20 minutes of your evening commute relaxing, so you can connect with your family once you're home.

- Live your core values. For instance, if being considerate is important to you but you're perpetually late for meetings, practice intentionally showing up five minutes early for meetings.

Steve Wanner is a highly respected 37-year-old partner at Ernst & Young, married with four young children. When I met him a year ago, he was working 12- to 14-hour days, felt perpetually exhausted, and found it difficult to fully engage with his family in the evenings, which left him feeling guilty and dissatisfied. He slept poorly, made no time to exercise, and seldom ate healthy meals, instead grabbing a bite to eat on the run or while working at his desk.

Wanner's experience is not uncommon. Most of us respond to rising demands in the workplace by putting in longer hours, which inevitably take a toll on us physically, mentally, and emotionally. That leads to declining levels of engagement, increasing levels of distraction, high turnover rates, and soaring medical costs among employees. My colleagues and I at the Energy Project have worked with thousands of leaders and managers in the course of doing consulting and coaching at large organizations during the past five years. With remarkable consistency, these executives tell us they're pushing themselves harder than ever to keep up and increasingly feel they are at a breaking point.

The core problem with working longer hours is that time is a finite resource. Energy is a different story. Defined in physics as the capacity to work, energy comes from four main wellsprings in human beings: the body, emotions, mind, and spirit. In each, energy can be systematically expanded and regularly renewed by establishing specific rituals—behaviors that are intentionally practiced and precisely scheduled, with the goal of making them unconscious and automatic as quickly as possible.

To effectively reenergize their workforces, organizations need to shift their emphasis from getting more out of people to investing more in them, so they are motivated—and able—to bring more of themselves to work every day. To recharge themselves, individuals need to recognize the costs of energy-depleting behaviors and then take responsibility for changing them, regardless of the circumstances they're facing.

The rituals and behaviors Wanner established to better manage his energy transformed his life. He set an earlier bedtime and gave up drinking, which had disrupted his sleep. As a consequence, when he woke up he felt more rested and more motivated to exercise, which he now does almost every morning. In less than two months he lost 15 pounds. After working out he now sits down with his family for breakfast. Wanner still puts in long hours on the job, but he renews himself regularly along the way. He leaves his desk for lunch and usually takes a morning and an afternoon walk outside. When he arrives at home in the evening, he's more relaxed and better able to connect with his wife and children.

Establishing simple rituals like these can lead to striking results across organizations. At Wachovia Bank, we took a group of employees through a pilot energy management program and then measured their performance against that of a control group. The participants outperformed the controls on a series of financial metrics, such as the value of loans they generated. They also reported substantial improvements in their customer relationships, their engagement with work, and their personal satisfaction. In this article, I'll describe the Wachovia study in a little more detail. Then I'll explain what executives and managers can do to increase and regularly renew work capacity—the approach used by the Energy Project, which builds on, deepens, and extends several core concepts developed by my former partner Jim Loehr in his seminal work with athletes.

Linking Capacity and Performance at Wachovia

Most large organizations invest in developing employees' skills, knowledge, and competence. Very few help build and sustain their capacity—their energy—which is typically taken for granted. In fact, greater capacity makes it possible to get more done in less time at a higher level of engagement and with more sustainability. Our experience at Wachovia bore this out.

In early 2006 we took 106 employees at 12 regional banks in southern New Jersey through a curriculum of four modules, each of which focused on specific strategies for strengthening one of the four main dimensions of energy. We delivered it at one-month intervals to groups of approximately 20 to 25, ranging from senior leaders to lower-level managers. We also assigned each attendee a fellow employee as a source of support between sessions. Using Wachovia's own key performance metrics, we evaluated how the participant group performed compared with a group of employees at similar levels at a nearby set of Wachovia banks who did not go through the training. To create a credible basis for comparison, we looked at year-over-year percentage changes in performance across several metrics.

On a measure called the "Big 3"—revenues from three kinds of loans—the participants showed a year-over-year increase that was 13 percentage points greater than the control group's in the first three months of our study. On revenues from deposits, the participants exceeded the control group's year-over-year gain by 20 percentage points during that same period. The precise gains varied month by month, but with only a handful of exceptions, the participants continued to significantly outperform the control group for a full year after completing the program. Although other variables undoubtedly influenced these outcomes, the participants' superior performance was notable in its consistency. (See figure 3-1.)

We also asked participants how the program influenced them personally. Sixty-eight percent reported that it had a positive impact on their relationships with clients and customers. Seventy-one percent said that it had a noticeable or substantial positive impact on their productivity and performance. These findings corroborated a raft of anecdotal evidence we've gathered about

FIGURE 3-1

How energy renewal programs boosted productivity at Wachovia

At Wachovia Bank, employees participating in an energy renewal program outperformed a control group of employees, demonstrating significantly greater improvements in year-over-year performance during the first quarter of 2006.

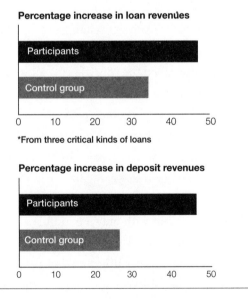

Percentage increase in loan revenues

Participants

Control group

0   10   20   30   40   50

*From three critical kinds of loans

Percentage increase in deposit revenues

Participants

Control group

0   10   20   30   40   50

the effectiveness of this approach among leaders at other large companies such as Ernst & Young, Sony, Deutsche Bank, Nokia, ING Direct, Ford, and MasterCard.

The Body: Physical Energy

Our program begins by focusing on physical energy. It is scarcely news that inadequate nutrition, exercise, sleep, and rest diminish people's basic energy levels, as well as their ability to manage their emotions and focus their attention. Nonetheless, many executives don't find ways to practice consistently healthy behaviors, given all the other demands in their lives.

Before participants in our program begin to explore ways to increase their physical energy, they take an energy audit, which includes four questions in each energy dimension—body, emotions, mind, and spirit. (See the sidebar "Are You Headed for an Energy Crisis?") On average, participants get eight to 10 of those 16 questions "wrong," meaning they're doing things such as skipping breakfast, failing to express appreciation to others, struggling to focus on one thing at a time, or spending too little time on activities that give them a sense of purpose. While most participants aren't surprised to learn these behaviors are counterproductive, having them all listed in one place is often uncomfortable, sobering, and galvanizing. The audit highlights employees' greatest energy deficits. Participants also fill out charts designed to raise their awareness about how their exercise, diet, and sleep practices influence their energy levels.

The next step is to identify rituals for building and renewing physical energy. When Gary Faro, a vice president

ARE YOU HEADED FOR AN ENERGY CRISIS?

Please check the statements below that are true for you.

Body

☐ I don't regularly get at least seven to eight hours of sleep, and I often wake up feeling tired.

☐ I frequently skip breakfast, or I settle for something that isn't nutritious.

☐ I don't work out enough (meaning cardiovascular training at least three times a week and strength training at least once a week).

☐ I don't take regular breaks during the day to truly renew and recharge, or I often eat lunch at my desk, if I eat it at all.

Emotions

☐ I frequently find myself feeling irritable, impatient, or anxious at work, especially when work is demanding.

☐ I don't have enough time with my family and loved ones, and when I'm with them, I'm not always really with them.

☐ I have too little time for the activities that I most deeply enjoy.

☐ I don't stop frequently enough to express my appreciation to others or to savor my accomplishments and blessings.

Mind

☐ I have difficulty focusing on one thing at a time, and I am easily distracted during the day, especially by e-mail.

☐ I spend much of my day reacting to immediate crises and demands rather than focusing on activities with longer-term value and high leverage.

☐ I don't take enough time for reflection, strategizing, and creative thinking.

☐ I work in the evenings or on weekends, and I almost never take an e-mail–free vacation.

Spirit

☐ I don't spend enough time at work doing what I do best and enjoy most.

☐ There are significant gaps between what I say is most important to me in my life and how I actually allocate my time and energy.

☐ My decisions at work are more often influenced by external demands than by a strong, clear sense of my own purpose.

☐ I don't invest enough time and energy in making a positive difference to others or to the world.

How Is Your Overall Energy?

Total number of statements checked: ___

ARE YOU HEADED FOR AN ENERGY CRISIS?

Guide to scores

0–3: Excellent energy management skills

4–6: Reasonable energy management skills

7–10: Significant energy management deficits

11–16: A full-fledged energy management crisis

What do you need to work on?

Number of checks in each category:

Body __

Mind __

Emotions __

Spirit __

Guide to category scores

0: Excellent energy management skills

1: Strong energy management skills

2: Significant deficits

3: Poor energy management skills

4: A full-fledged energy crisis

at Wachovia, began the program, he was significantly overweight, ate poorly, lacked a regular exercise routine, worked long hours, and typically slept no more than five or six hours a night. That is not an unusual profile among the leaders and managers we see. Over the course of the program, Faro began regular cardiovascular and strength training. He started going to bed at a designated time and sleeping longer. He changed his eating habits from two big meals a day ("Where I usually gorged myself," he says) to smaller meals and light snacks every three hours. The aim was to help him stabilize his glucose levels over the course of the day, avoiding peaks and valleys. He lost 50 pounds in the process, and his energy levels soared. "I used to schedule tough projects for the morning, when I knew that I would be more focused," Faro says. "I don't have to do that anymore because I find that I'm just as focused now at 5 PM as I am at 8 AM."

Another key ritual Faro adopted was to take brief but regular breaks at specific intervals throughout the workday—always leaving his desk. The value of such breaks is grounded in our physiology. "Ultradian rhythms" refer to 90- to 120-minute cycles during which our bodies slowly move from a high-energy state into a physiological trough. Toward the end of each cycle, the body begins to crave a period of recovery. The signals include physical restlessness, yawning, hunger, and difficulty concentrating, but many of us ignore them and keep working. The consequence is that our energy reservoir—our remaining capacity—burns down as the day wears on.

Intermittent breaks for renewal, we have found, result in higher and more sustainable performance. The length of renewal is less important than the quality. It is possible to get a great deal of recovery in a short time—as little as several minutes—if it involves a ritual that allows you to disengage from work and truly change channels. That could range from getting up to talk to a colleague about something other than work, to listening to music on an iPod, to walking up and down stairs in an office building. While breaks are countercultural in most organizations

GROWN-UPS NEED RECESS, TOO

Taking time out of your workday to restore and rejuvenate yourself seems like a guilty pleasure. After all, shouldn't you be doing something to reduce costs or increase revenue? But our research for Wharton's Work/Life Integration Project shows that small breaks actually *improve* performance because you bring stronger, more focused effort to your work after fruitful rest—just as kids do after recess time in school.

What might this look like in practice? Here are a few examples:

- Turn off your mobile devices for 30 minutes each day, whenever works best. Just shutting off the stream of texts, instant messages, and calls counts as a break.

- Work out with a friend or coworker one morning a week.

- Set aside 15 minutes a day during your commute or coffee break to read something fun, do a crossword puzzle, or chat with a friend.

- Start a monthly book or puzzle swap with your colleagues.

- Find five minutes—and an empty conference room—to do jumping jacks or some light stretching.

How do you take time out in ways you can sustain? Here are some tips:

1. *Try small steps.* You're much more likely to keep it up if "recess" doesn't require a big restructuring of your life.

2. *List the benefits—direct or indirect—to others.* Maybe you feel less distracted at work, for example, or approach teamwork with more patience. If you think about what your coworkers are getting out of your improved outlook, you'll feel less guilty about doing something that at first might seem selfish.

3. *Enroll someone you trust to serve as your coach.* It can be anyone, as long as he or she provides both support and accountability pressure.

4. *Get feedback after a week or two.* Ask people at work if, indeed, you're better serving their needs and interests as a result of taking your recess and feeling refreshed. Adjust as you learn what's working—and what's not—from others' perspective.

Adapted from content posted on hbr.org by Stewart D. Friedman on February 25, 2009

and counterintuitive for many high achievers, their value is multifaceted.

Matthew Lang is a managing director for Sony in South Africa. He adopted some of the same rituals that Faro did, including a 20-minute walk in the afternoons. Lang's walk not only gives him a mental and emotional breather and some exercise but also has become the time when he gets his best creative ideas. That's because when he walks, he is not actively thinking, which allows the dominant left hemisphere of his brain to give way to the right hemisphere with its greater capacity to see the big picture and make imaginative leaps.

The Emotions: Quality of Energy

When people are able to take more control of their emotions, they can improve the quality of their energy, regardless of the external pressures they're facing. To do this, they first must become more aware of how they feel at various points during the workday and of the impact these emotions have on their effectiveness. Most people realize that they tend to perform best when they're feeling positive energy. What they find surprising is that they're not able to perform well or to lead effectively when they're feeling any other way.

Unfortunately, without intermittent recovery, we're not physiologically capable of sustaining highly positive emotions for long periods. Confronted with relentless demands and unexpected challenges, people tend to slip into negative emotions—the fight-or-flight mode—often multiple times in a day. They become irritable and impatient, or anxious and insecure. Such states of mind drain people's energy and cause friction in their relationships. Fight-or-flight emotions also make it impossible to think clearly, logically, and reflectively. When executives learn to recognize what kinds of events trigger their negative emotions, they gain greater capacity to take control of their reactions.

One simple but powerful ritual for defusing negative emotions is what we call "buying time." Deep abdominal breathing is one way to do that. Exhaling slowly for five or six seconds induces relaxation and recovery, and turns off the fight-or-flight response. When we began working with Fujio Nishida, president of Sony Europe, he had a habit of lighting up a cigarette each time something especially stressful occurred—at least two or three times a day. Otherwise, he didn't smoke. We taught him the breathing exercise as an alternative, and it worked immediately: Nishida found he no longer had the desire for a cigarette. It wasn't the smoking that had given him relief from the stress, we concluded, but the relaxation prompted by the deep inhalation and exhalation.

A powerful ritual that fuels positive emotions is expressing appreciation to others, a practice that seems to be as beneficial to the giver as to the receiver. It can take the form of a handwritten note, an e-mail, a call, or a conversation—and the more detailed and specific, the higher the impact. As with all rituals, setting aside a particular time to do it vastly increases the chances of success. Ben Jenkins, vice chairman and president of the General Bank at Wachovia in Charlotte, North Carolina, built his appreciation ritual into time set aside for mentoring. He began scheduling lunches or dinners regularly with people who worked for him. Previously, the only sit-downs he'd had with his direct reports were to hear monthly reports on their numbers or to give them yearly performance reviews. Now, over meals, he makes it a priority to recognize their accomplishments and also to talk with them about their lives and their aspirations rather than their immediate work responsibilities.

Finally, people can cultivate positive emotions by learning to change the stories they tell themselves about the events in their lives. Often, people in conflict cast themselves in the role of victim, blaming others or external circumstances for their problems. Becoming aware of the difference between the facts in a given situation and the way we interpret those facts can be powerful in itself. It's been a revelation for many of the people we work with to discover they have a choice about how to view a given event and to recognize how powerfully the story they tell influences the emotions they feel. We teach them to tell the most hopeful and personally empowering story possible in any given situation, without denying or minimizing the facts.

The most effective way people can change a story is to view it through any of three new lenses, which are all alternatives to seeing the world from the victim perspective. With the *reverse lens,* for example, people ask themselves, "What would the other person in this conflict say and in what ways might that be true?" With the *long lens* they ask, "How will I most likely view this situation in six months?" With the *wide lens* they ask themselves, "Regardless of the outcome of this issue, how can I grow and learn from it?" Each of these lenses can help people intentionally cultivate more positive emotions.

Nicolas Babin, director of corporate communications for Sony Europe, was the point person for calls from reporters when Sony went through several recalls of its batteries in 2006. Over time he found his work increasingly exhausting and dispiriting. After practicing the lens exercises, he began finding ways to tell himself a more positive and empowering story about his role. "I realized," he explains, "that this was an opportunity for me to build stronger relationships with journalists by being accessible to them and to increase Sony's credibility by being straightforward and honest."

The Mind: Focus of Energy

Many executives view multitasking as a necessity in the face of all the demands they juggle, but it actually undermines productivity. Distractions are costly: A temporary shift in attention from one task to another—stopping to answer an e-mail or take a phone call, for instance—increases the amount of time necessary to finish the primary task by as much as 25%, a phenomenon known as "switching time." It's far more efficient to fully focus for 90 to 120 minutes, take a true break, and then fully focus on the next activity. We refer to these work periods as "ultradian sprints."

Once people see how much they struggle to concentrate, they can create rituals to reduce the relentless interruptions that technology has introduced in their lives. We start out with an exercise that forces them to face the impact of daily distractions. They attempt to complete a complex task and are regularly interrupted—an experience that, people report, ends up feeling much like everyday life.

Dan Cluna, a vice president at Wachovia, designed two rituals to better focus his attention. The first one is to leave his desk and go into a conference room, away from phones and e-mail, whenever he has a task that requires concentration. He now finishes reports in a third of the time they used to require. Cluna built his second ritual around meetings at branches with the financial specialists who report to him. Previously, he would answer his phone whenever it rang during these meetings. As a consequence, the meetings he scheduled for an hour often stretched to two, and he rarely gave anyone his full attention. Now Cluna lets his phone go to voice mail so that he can focus completely on the person in front of him. He now answers the accumulated voice-mail messages when he has downtime between meetings.

E&Y's hard-charging Wanner used to answer e-mail constantly throughout the day—whenever he heard a "ping." Then he created a ritual of checking his e-mail just twice a day—at 10:15 AM and 2:30 PM. Whereas previously he couldn't keep up with all his messages, he discovered he could clear his in-box each time he opened it—the reward of fully focusing his attention on e-mail for 45 minutes at a time. Wanner has also reset the expectations of all the people he regularly communicates with by e-mail. "I've told them if it's an emergency and they need an instant response, they can call me and I'll always pick up," he says. Nine months later he has yet to receive such a call.

Michael Henke, a senior manager at E&Y, sat his team down at the start of the busy season last winter and told them that at certain points during the day he was going to turn off his Sametime (an in-house instant-message system). The result, he said, was that he would be less available to them for questions. Like Wanner, he told his team to call him if any emergency arose, but they rarely did. He also encouraged the group to take regular breaks throughout the day and to eat more regularly. They finished the busy season under budget and more profitable than other teams that hadn't followed the energy renewal program. "We got the same amount of work done in less time," says Henke. "It made for a win-win."

Another way to mobilize mental energy is to focus systematically on activities that have the most long-term leverage. Unless people intentionally schedule time for more challenging work, they tend not to get to it at all or rush through it at the last minute. Perhaps the most effective focus ritual the executives we work with have adopted is to identify each night the most important challenge for the next day and make it their very first priority when they arrive in the morning. Jean Luc Duquesne, a vice president for Sony Europe in Paris, used to answer his e-mail as soon as he got to the office, just as many people do. He now tries to concentrate the first hour of every day on the most important topic. He finds that he often emerges at 10 AM feeling as if he's already had a productive day.

The Human Spirit: Energy of Meaning and Purpose

People tap into the energy of the human spirit when their everyday work and activities are consistent with what they value most and with what gives them a sense of meaning and purpose. If the work they're doing really matters to them, they typically feel more positive energy, focus better, and demonstrate greater perseverance. Regrettably, the high demands and fast pace of corporate life don't leave much time to pay attention to these issues, and many people don't even recognize meaning and purpose as potential sources of energy. Indeed, if we tried to begin our program by focusing on the human spirit, it would likely have minimal impact. Only when participants have experienced the value of the rituals they establish in the other dimensions do they start to see that being attentive to their own deeper needs dramatically influences their effectiveness and satisfaction at work.

For E&Y partner Jonathan Anspacher, simply having the opportunity to ask himself a series of questions about what really mattered to him was both illuminating and energizing. "I think it's important to be a little introspective and say, 'What do you want to be remembered for?'" he told us. "You don't want to be remembered as the crazy partner who worked these long hours and had his people be miserable. When my kids call me and ask, 'Can you come to my band concert?' I want to say, 'Yes, I'll be there and I'll be in the front row.' I don't want to be the father that comes in and sits in the back and is on his Black-Berry and has to step out to take a phone call."

To access the energy of the human spirit, people need to clarify priorities and establish accompanying rituals in three categories: doing what they do best and enjoy most at work; consciously allocating time and energy to the areas of their lives—work, family, health, service to others—they deem most important; and living their core values in their daily behaviors.

When you're attempting to discover what you do best and what you enjoy most, it's important to realize that these two things aren't necessarily mutually inclusive. You may get lots of positive feedback about something you're very good at but not truly enjoy it. Conversely, you can love doing something but have no gift for it, so that achieving success requires much more energy than it makes sense to invest.

To help program participants discover their areas of strength, we ask them to recall at least two work experiences in the past several months during which they found themselves in their "sweet spot"—feeling effective, effortlessly absorbed, inspired, and fulfilled. Then we have them deconstruct those experiences to understand precisely what energized them so positively and what specific talents they were drawing on. If leading strategy feels like a sweet spot, for example, is it being in charge that's most invigorating or participating in a creative endeavor? Or is it using a skill that comes to you easily and so feels good to exercise? Finally, we have people establish a ritual that will encourage them to do more of exactly that kind of activity at work.

A senior leader we worked with realized that one of the activities he least liked was reading and summarizing detailed sales reports, whereas one of his favorites was brainstorming new strategies. The leader found a direct report who loved immersing himself in numbers and delegated the sales report task to him—happily settling for brief oral summaries from him each day. The leader also began scheduling a free-form 90-minute strategy session every other week with the most creative people in his group.

In the second category, devoting time and energy to what's important to you, there is often a similar divide between what people say is important and what they actually do. Rituals can help close this gap. When Jean Luc Duquesne, the Sony Europe vice president, thought hard about his personal priorities, he realized that spending time with his family was what mattered most to him, but it often got squeezed out of his day. So he instituted a ritual in which he switches off for at least three hours every evening when he gets home, so he can focus on his family. "I'm still not an expert on PlayStation," he told us, "but according to my youngest son, I'm learning and I'm a good student." Steve Wanner, who used to talk on the cell phone all the way to his front door on his commute home, has chosen a specific spot 20 minutes from his house where he ends whatever call he's on and puts away the phone. He spends the rest of his commute relaxing so that when he does arrive home, he's less preoccupied with work and more available to his wife and children.

The third category, practicing your core values in your everyday behavior, is a challenge for many as well. Most people are living at such a furious pace that they rarely stop to ask themselves what they stand for and who they want to be. As a consequence, they let external demands dictate their actions.

We don't suggest that people explicitly define their values, because the results are usually too predictable.

Instead, we seek to uncover them, in part by asking questions that are inadvertently revealing, such as, "What are the qualities that you find most off-putting when you see them in others?" By describing what they can't stand, people unintentionally divulge what they stand for. If you are very offended by stinginess, for example, generosity is probably one of your key values. If you are especially put off by rudeness in others, it's likely that consideration is a high value for you. As in the other categories, establishing rituals can help bridge the gap between the values you aspire to and how you currently behave. If you discover that consideration is a key value, but you are perpetually late for meetings, the ritual might be to end the meetings you run five minutes earlier than usual and intentionally show up five minutes early for the meeting that follows.

Addressing these three categories helps people go a long way toward achieving a greater sense of alignment, satisfaction, and well-being in their lives on and off the job. Those feelings are a source of positive energy in their own right and reinforce people's desire to persist at rituals in other energy dimensions as well.

This new way of working takes hold only to the degree that organizations support their people in adopting new behaviors. We have learned, sometimes painfully, that not all executives and companies are prepared to embrace the notion that personal renewal for employees will lead to better and more sustainable performance. To succeed, renewal efforts need solid support and commitment from senior management, beginning with the key decision maker.

At Wachovia, Susanne Svizeny, the president of the region in which we conducted our study, was the primary cheerleader for the program. She embraced the principles in her own life and made a series of personal changes, including a visible commitment to building more regular renewal rituals into her work life. Next, she took it upon herself to foster the excitement and commitment of her leadership team. Finally, she regularly reached out by e-mail to all participants in the project to encourage them in their rituals and seek their feedback. It was clear to everyone that she took the work seriously. Her enthusiasm was infectious, and the results spoke for themselves.

At Sony Europe, several hundred leaders have embraced the principles of energy management. Over the next year, more than 2,000 of their direct reports will go through the energy renewal program. From Fujio Nishida on down, it has become increasingly culturally acceptable at Sony to take intermittent breaks, work out at midday, answer e-mail only at designated times, and even ask colleagues who seem irritable or impatient what stories they're telling themselves.

Organizational support also entails shifts in policies, practices, and cultural messages. A number of firms we worked with have built "renewal rooms" where people can regularly go to relax and refuel. Others offer subsidized gym memberships. In some cases, leaders themselves gather groups of employees for midday workouts. One company instituted a no-meeting zone between 8 and 9 AM to ensure that people had at least one hour absolutely free of meetings. At several companies, including Sony, senior leaders collectively agreed to stop checking e-mail during meetings as a way to make the meetings more focused and efficient.

One factor that can get in the way of success is a crisis mentality. The optimal candidates for energy renewal programs are organizations that are feeling enough pain to be eager for new solutions but not so much that they're completely overwhelmed. At one organization where we had the active support of the CEO, the company was under intense pressure to grow rapidly, and the senior team couldn't tear themselves away from their focus on immediate survival—even though taking time out for renewal might have allowed them to be more productive at a more sustainable level.

By contrast, the group at Ernst & Young successfully went through the process at the height of tax season. With the permission of their leaders, they practiced defusing negative emotions by breathing or telling themselves different stories, and alternated highly focused periods of work with renewal breaks. Most people in the group reported that this busy season was the least stressful they'd ever experienced.

The implicit contract between organizations and their employees today is that each will try to get as much from the other as they can, as quickly as possible, and then move on without looking back. We believe that is mutually self-defeating. Both individuals and the organizations they work for end up depleted rather than enriched. Employees feel increasingly beleaguered and burned out. Organizations are forced to settle for employees who are less than fully engaged and to constantly hire and train new people to replace those who choose to leave. We envision a new and explicit contract that benefits all parties: Organizations invest in their people across all dimensions of their lives to help them build and sustain their value. Individuals respond by bringing all their multidimensional energy wholeheartedly to work every day. Both grow in value as a result.

———————

Tony Schwartz is the president and founder of The Energy Project in New York City, and a coauthor of *The Power of Full Engagement: Managing Energy, Not Time, Is the Key to High Performance and Personal Renewal* (Free Press, 2003). **Catherine McCarthy** is a senior vice president at The Energy Project.

Chapter 4
Why Great Performers Sleep More

by Tony Schwartz

Why is sleep one of the first things we're willing to sacrifice as the demands in our lives keep rising? We continue to live by a remarkably durable myth: Sleeping one hour less will give us one more hour of productivity. In reality, even small amounts of sleep deprivation take a significant toll on our health, mood, cognitive capacity, and productivity.

How Much Sleep Do You Need?

When researchers put test subjects into environments without clocks or windows and ask them to sleep any

---

Adapted from content posted on hbr.org on March 3, 2011

time they feel tired, 95% sleep between seven and eight hours out of every 24. Another 2.5% sleep more than eight hours. That means just 2.5% of us require fewer than seven hours of sleep a night to feel fully rested. That's one out of every 40 people.

In my talks, when I ask who has had fewer than seven hours of sleep several nights during the past week, the majority raise their hands. That's true whether it's an audience of corporate executives, teachers, cops, or government workers.

Great performers are an exception. Typically, they sleep significantly *more* than the rest of us. In Anders Ericsson's famous study of violinists, the top performers slept an average of eight and a half hours out of every 24, including a 20- to 30-minute midafternoon nap—some two hours a day more than the average American.

The top violinists also reported that except for practice itself, sleep was the most important factor in improving their skills.

As I gathered research about sleep, I felt increasingly compelled to give it higher priority in my own life. Today, I go to great lengths to ensure that I get at least eight hours every night, and ideally between eight and a half and nine hours, even when I'm traveling.

I still take the overnight red-eye from California to New York, but I'm asleep by takeoff—even if I have to take a sleeping aid. When I get home at 6:00 or 7:00 AM, I go right to bed until I've had my eight hours. What I've learned about those days is that I'd rather work at 100% for five or six hours than at 60% for eight or nine hours.

WHAT PEOPLE ARE SAYING ON HBR.ORG

Try the coffee nap—Lifehacker had a great article about [naps]. I'm a paramedic and I've used this trick for ages. Fix a cup of coffee so you can drink it quickly. Set up the spot where you'll nap and then drink the coffee. Set a timer for 20 minutes and make sure you get up when it goes off. Any longer and you'll feel worn out. I know this has saved my life on many late-night, long-distance transports. —Posted by John

With sufficient sleep, I feel better, I work with more focus, and I manage my emotions better, which is good for everyone around me. I dislike enduring even a single day when I haven't had enough sleep because the impact is immediate and unavoidable. On the rare days that I don't get enough, I try hard to get at least a 20- to 30-minute nap in the afternoon. That's a big help.

How to Get More Sleep

Here are three other tips to improve the quantity and quality of your sleep:

- **Write down what's on your mind before you get into bed.** If you leave items such as unfinished to-do's and unresolved issues in your working memory, they'll make it harder to fall asleep, and you'll end up ruminating about them if you wake up during the night.

- **Go to bed earlier—and at a set time.** Sounds obvious, right? The problem is there's no alternative. You're already waking up at the latest possible time you can. If you don't ritualize a specific bedtime, you'll find ways to stay up later, just the way you do now.

- **Start winding down at least 45 minutes before you turn out the light.** You won't fall asleep if you're all wound up from answering e-mail or doing other work. Create a ritual around drinking a cup of herbal tea, listening to music that helps you relax, or reading a dull book.

Tony Schwartz is the president and CEO of The Energy Project and the author of *Be Excellent at Anything* (Free Press, 2011). Become a fan of The Energy Project on Facebook and connect with Tony on Twitter at @tonyschwartz and @energy_project.

Section 3
Improving Your Work/Life Balance

Chapter 5
No, You Can't Have It All

by Eric C. Sinoway

Imagine that a company needs two volunteers for a high-profile, out-of-town project. Who should go? Everyone has pressures and commitments to consider. There's the young manager eager for his next promotion but worried about leaving his wife at home with their toddler and newborn son; the rising star who's already juggling long hours at work, a part-time MBA program, and the planning of her wedding; the mid-career executive who just joined a nonprofit board and doesn't want to miss his first meeting; the single colleague who would relish the assignment but is about to move her father into a nursing home; and an overweight team member with a family

Reprinted from *Harvard Business Review*, October 2012 (product #R1210J)

history of diabetes who knows the travel will cause him to blow his new diet and exercise routine.

Platitudes about the importance of work–life balance don't fully capture the complexity of those employees' situations. The pursuit of a meaningful, multifaceted life involves endless choices about both short-term tactical issues ("Should I volunteer for this project?") and long-term strategic ones ("How can I position myself to advance in my career?"). Howard Stevenson is an entrepreneur, professor, philanthropist, former chairman of Harvard Business Publishing, husband, and father who has spent four decades studying, teaching, and advising leaders in all types of organizations. He likens the challenge to walking on a balance beam while trying to juggle an egg, a crystal glass, a knife, and any number of other fragile or hazardous objects. As you progress in your career and life, more responsibilities and opportunities are tossed at you. And so at some point, to maintain your balance, you'll have to drop something. The key is to decide consciously what to relinquish instead of unwittingly letting go of the most important item.

It's hard for high-achieving people to accept that they can't have it all. Even those who recognize the limits on their time often still expect to be energetic and efficient enough to excel in every role: productive employee, inspiring boss and mentor, supportive colleague, active community member, and committed spouse, friend, parent, and child. It's a natural response to our upbringings; after all, in school we're taught that hardworking, intelligent students can get straight A's. But in the messy real world, it is impossible to do everything perfectly at the same time. You cannot pursue all your goals simultaneously or satisfy all your desires at once. And it's an emotional drain to think you can. Instead, you must focus on long-term fulfillment rather than short-term success and, at various points in your life, think carefully about your priorities.

This article presents a framework that I have developed in collaboration with Howard. It's based on his experience teaching and mentoring students and on the lessons I've learned navigating my own career and now running Axcess Worldwide. The framework is designed to help people—particularly ambitious executives—understand their limits and make the tough trade-offs that can lead to more-satisfying careers and lives.

You, the Ongoing Process

We all know that it's difficult for a company to make good strategic or tactical decisions without a mission in mind. The same holds true for individuals. Think of a jigsaw puzzle: It's much easier to put the pieces together if you look at the front of the box. But life does not come with a picture that shows what success looks like. Most of us start walking and juggling on the balance beam without thinking holistically and explicitly about what aspects of our lives we value most and how we value those things in relation to one another. Those assessments are not easy, but they are central to defining your goals and your desired legacy. It helps to carefully consider all the dimensions of your life. Howard and I have identified seven:

- Family (parents, children, siblings, in-laws, and so on)

- Social and community (friendships and community engagement)

- Spiritual (religion, philosophy, or emotional outlook)

- Physical (health and well-being)

- Material (physical environment and possessions)

- Avocational (hobbies and other nonprofessional activities)

- Career (both short- and long-term perspectives)

For each dimension ask yourself three questions: Who do I want to be in this part of my life? How much do I want to experience this dimension? Given that I have a finite amount of time, energy, and resources, how important is this dimension relative to the others?

As you consider the answers, it's important to recognize two points. First, each dimension presents distinct challenges. It's crucial to tease them apart so that you are facing not an overwhelming whole but discrete issues that can be addressed individually. Second, your evaluation can and will change. The idea is to develop an aspirational picture of yourself for the present and a legacy vision for the future as a guide for deciding how to spend your personal resources. This is especially important when you feel you're losing your balance or are about to fumble.

Two of Howard's own life experiences offer potent examples of how to use this aspirational vision to shape decisions both large and small. The first is from the time when he was building Baupost—the money management firm he cofounded—as well as teaching at Harvard Business School. At that point, he couldn't spend as much time as he would have liked with his young children, because he was working long hours and traveling a lot. The situation reflected clear decisions he and his wife had made: He would sacrifice the family dimension of his life for a while in order to create the best long-term outcome for all of them. But Howard employed a tactical fix that honored his vision of himself as a committed husband and father. Whenever he was at home, he was fully responsive. Regardless of what else he was doing—catching up on work, reading a book, cleaning out the garage—if one of his family members asked for help with something or just wanted to talk, he would stop and engage. He knew that the emotional value from the interaction—for him and his family—would be far higher than the value of any other task. He applied clear-headed analysis to an important challenge: how to be a good father, husband, and provider while maximizing the professional dimension of his life.

Several years later, when Howard was in his late 40s and thriving at both Baupost and Harvard, he faced a much more complicated set of choices when his marriage ended. He realized he could regain his own and his sons' equilibrium only by rechanneling personal resources from his career to his family. And so he gave up his leadership role at Baupost—a job he loved, and one

CAN YOU REALLY ACHIEVE YOUR GOAL?

Before trying to pursue a significant goal, especially a professional one, it's important to assess whether you have the ability to achieve it. Consider two things:

1. Do you have the required core capacities: knowledge, skills, and personal characteristics?

2. Are your capacities as good as or better than those of other people with the same goal?

If you answer no to either question, you should consider revising your goal. If you answer yes to both, make sure you're not succumbing to one of these five common fallacies:

The hard-work fallacy: believing that determined effort will compensate for your shortcomings

The smarts fallacy: thinking that general intelligence translates into specific skills

The magnification fallacy: assuming that your particular talent is somehow more special than your peers'

The passion fallacy: believing you're good at things just because you really enjoy them or because they are immensely important to you

The "wishing will make it so" fallacy: convincing yourself that success (for you, anyway) will be easy

that might have given him an income in the tens of millions of dollars. "I needed to earn a consistently good grade as a father for an extended period," he explained. "I couldn't risk having some aspect of my family responsibilities slip through my fingers. Sure, my ego and my wallet both took big hits. But the value of having more time and energy for my kids far outweighed any incremental monetary value."

Assessing Value

Notice that in describing his experiences, Howard used the word "value." That's because he's an entrepreneur who knows that the only way to truly assess cost is to understand the value of one choice relative to another. For example, an hour spent reading to your daughter has a different value than an hour spent playing basketball with friends; and both have values different from an hour spent studying for a licensing exam or volunteering at a homeless shelter. The key is to differentiate between options that appear to be equally valuable by carefully considering how each of them advances you toward one dimension or another of your legacy vision. The following questions can help you in that process.

Where do your options fall on the needs–wants spectrum?

Needs start with food, shelter, and health; wants include diamond necklaces, round-the-world cruises, and mansions. Needs have more intrinsic value than wants. But most things fall somewhere in the middle. So the goal is to understand, in relative terms, where your options fall on the spectrum, based on your individual circumstances at a given moment and on your legacy vision. Some wants are so strong—because of habit or even peer pressure—that it's difficult to separate them from needs.

Consider two examples. (In these and the cases of Willie and Andrew, below, names and some personal details have been changed out of respect for the subjects' privacy.) The first concerns a college classmate, Carin, who gets very sad if she can't take time each day to play the piano; the hobby is so much a part of who she wants to be that it has become, in practical terms, a need, so she sacrifices in other dimensions of her life to make time for it. The second involves two former colleagues, Irwin and Bill, who work at the same firm. Both were considering buying an expensive car and a handmade Swiss watch—investments that would consume significant amounts of cash and curtail their 401(k) contributions. For Irwin, a 29-year-old trying to impress his peers, these purchases were largely wants. But for Bill, a 46-year-old who had been promoted to a senior role in the luxury division of the company and was routinely entertaining wealthy clients, the car and the watch were closer to needs: He had to present himself in a certain way to be successful.

What are the investment and opportunity costs?

Almost every decision—whether agreeing to a strategic business alliance or committing to a leadership role in a nonprofit organization—involves two kinds of costs. There's the investment cost: the time, energy, and other resources you expend. And there's the opportunity cost:

the options you forgo by investing those resources. The challenge with investment costs is to be explicit about them up front and to understand if and how incurring them will lead you to your desired, well-defined outcome.

For example, rather than blindly diving into a full-scale job search to explore new career options, which would represent a very large investment of time and energy, you can commit to spending just five hours a week for two months researching a few industries you find promising, networking with contacts who know them, and doing informational interviews with executives working in them. The goal might be to create a short list of 10 companies where you'd like to work and to pinpoint three to five roles you'd like to play at them. At the same time, be sure to weigh your opportunity costs: what you won't be able to do because you're spending five hours a week on the job search. Perhaps you'll have to stop playing in the after-work softball league or decline to participate in a new cross-division initiative at your current workplace.

Are the potential benefits worth the costs?

Expected benefits must be evaluated just as carefully as costs, and in relation to them. Does the benefit you'll receive warrant the investment you'll have to make? The songwriter Lucy Kaplansky captures this idea succinctly: "How much did it cost you? How much did you pay? And are you sorry at the end of the day?" Willie, a friend who works for a large conglomerate, was recently told by his boss that he would be well served to earn his CPA, an achievement that requires three years of coursework. "Well served" implies a benefit, but how much of one?

Would he get a promotion or a raise after earning his CPA? If so, to what level? Would he be eligible to move to other divisions in the company? If so, which ones? Willie has to answer those questions in order to decide whether the costs of this particular effort would produce acceptable returns.

Can you make a trade?

Life is full of trade-offs, but sometimes units of one element of your life can't be exchanged for units of a different element. Think of Steve Jobs, who assuredly would have paid great sums to cure his cancer. But his money could not buy him health. There was no trade to be had. Many of us face similar, albeit less consequential, challenges throughout our careers and lives as we try to exchange something we have for something else that we want. The frustration arises when the two items in question can't be traded.

Consider the case of Andrew, a managing director at a respected financial services firm. He'd spent nearly 20 years in investment banking, but thanks to the unsteady economy, the demonization of his profession, and increased regulation, he was no longer enjoying his work. He'd long dreamed of walking away from financial services and opening a small beachside restaurant, and so, at age 52, he resigned. The firm offered him a staggering sum to stay, provided he commit to a five-year contract. After a few days of consideration, Andrew agreed, but now, two years later, he's miserable and still thinking about his restaurant. He ended up exchanging wealth for freedom, and although the money seemed very big and the freedom to be gained from his new endeavor relatively small, in the end it was a bad trade.

Can you pursue your most important goals sequentially?

Howard is fond of citing a piece of advice his mother often gave him: "Remember that you may be able to have everything you want in life—just not all at once." Consciously staggering your goals may enable you to be equally successful in many dimensions over time. Mike Leven, the 74-year-old president and COO of Las Vegas Sands, has said that he decided to focus on his work dimension later than his peers, because he wanted to be a more hands-on parent when his three children were young. So he reached professional goals at 45 that many friends reached at 40; achieved wealth later than others; and secured his first really big job, as the president of Days Inn, when his kids were a bit older. He didn't slack off in the early part of his career, but he did give himself permission to pursue his top personal and professional goals—of being a great father and a successful corporate leader—at different points in his life, because he believed he couldn't achieve them simultaneously.

In today's complex, frenetic world, many of us are—like the employees described at the start of this article—struggling to chart a path toward success in our careers and a sense of fulfillment in all aspects of our lives. Any decision can be easier if you think carefully about your goals; the dimensions of yourself that are most important to you; your needs and wants; the specific costs and benefits associated with your choices; the commensurability of those choices; and whether certain goals should be sequenced instead of pursued simultaneously to give you a better chance of success. Instead of striving for work–life balance, or even worrying about juggling on the balance beam, use this framework to pursue your life's work—holistically seeking both success and satisfaction. In the real world, isn't that what "having it all" really comes down to?

———————

Eric C. Sinoway is the president and a cofounder of Axcess Worldwide, which creates partnerships between companies in the luxury, travel, hospitality, and mass consumer brand industries. He is the author, with Merrill Meadow, of *Howard's Gift: Uncommon Wisdom to Inspire Your Life's Work* (St. Martin's Press, 2012).

Chapter 6
Making Time Off Predictable— and Required

by Leslie A. Perlow and Jessica L. Porter

IDEA IN BRIEF

- People in professional services believe a 24/7 work ethic is essential for getting ahead, and so they work 60-plus hours a week and are slaves to their BlackBerrys.

- The authors' research in several offices of the Boston Consulting Group, however, suggests that consultants and other professionals can meet the

Reprinted from *Harvard Business Review*, October 2009 (product #R0910M) highest standards of service and still have planned, uninterrupted time off—whether in good economic times or bad.

- Here's how: Impose a strict mechanism for taking time off, encourage lots of talk about what's working and what isn't, promote experimentation with different ways of working, and ensure top-level support.

People in professional services (consultants, investment bankers, accountants, lawyers, IT, and the like) simply expect to make work their top priority. They believe an "always on" ethic is essential if they and their firms are to succeed in the global marketplace. Just look at the numbers: According to a survey we conducted last year, 94% of 1,000 such professionals said they put in 50 or more hours a week, with nearly half that group turning in more than 65 hours a week. That doesn't include the 20 to 25 hours a week most of them spend monitoring their BlackBerrys while outside the office. These individuals further say they almost always respond within an hour of receiving a message from a colleague or a client.

Yet our research over the past four years in several North American offices of the Boston Consulting Group (BCG) suggests that it is perfectly possible for consultants and other professionals to meet the highest standards of service and still have planned, uninterrupted time off. Indeed, we found that when the assumption that everyone needs to be always available was collectively challenged, not only could individuals take time off, but their work actually benefited. Our experiments with time off resulted in more open dialogue among team members, which is valuable in itself. But the improved communication also sparked new processes that enhanced the teams' ability to work most efficiently and effectively.

Predictable time off is the name we gave to the designated periods of time that consultants were required to take off. This was in addition to time the consultants took off with the natural ebbs and flows of their work. These predictable periods were established at the start of a project and required individuals to be off completely—no checking of e-mail or voicemail. The concept was so foreign that we had to practically force some professionals to take their time off, especially when it coincided with periods of peak work intensity. Eventually, however, the consultants came to enjoy and anticipate having predictable time off, particularly as the benefits for their work became evident.

After we had conducted more than 10 multi-month time-off experiments at BCG, the effects of the recession became sharply apparent. The time pressures on service professionals proved even greater in this period of collapse—a fact borne out in a survey we recently conducted with an additional 250 individuals across professional services firms: 66% of respondents reported increased pressure in their work life, and 36% reported a significant increase.

When faced with sobering bottom-line effects of the recession, leaders at BCG paused to discuss and reconsider the benefits of implementing predictable time off—and decided to go ahead with this counterintuitive approach to increasing their efficiency and effectiveness. The payoff, they feel, is about far more than individual gains; it's about preserving a strong, engaged pool of talent and, ultimately, cultivating productive work processes for the long term.

To understand how effective predictable time off can be (in good times and bad), let's look at the experiments we conducted at BCG.

Rethinking the Unthinkable

The demands of consulting projects vary a great deal depending on multiple dimensions, including the scope of work promised, the type of relationship with the client, and the travel required. So in our first experiment, we made sure that our test was rigorous. We deliberately chose a team of four consultants who were working with a new client that BCG very much wanted to cultivate. The project involved a lot of daily interaction with the client, leading the consultants to believe that their presence at the client site four days a week was imperative. We imposed a requirement that everyone on the team take one full day off a week. Since that meant everyone was now working 80%, we added another consultant to the team to ensure that the client would still have the equivalent of four full-time people on the project.

At first, the team resisted the experiment. The partner in charge, who had been very supportive of the basic idea, was suddenly nervous about having to tell her client that each member of her team would be off one day a week. The project manager was also concerned: He was responsible for the team's final output, and he feared that the experiment might affect the quality of the team's work. However, both reluctantly agreed to give the experiment a try. Their reasoning was that since their firm had been hired to help the client improve its work processes (of the sales force, in this case), they could position the experiment as their own attempt to do what they were asking of their client—namely, engage in process improvement. They assured the client that they would call off the experiment if there were any cause for concern. The client was receptive.

This first experiment tested predictable time off at an extreme level because consultants were required to take off a full day, in the middle of the work week. As a partner put it, "Forcing a full day off was like tying your right hand behind your back to teach you to use your left hand. It really helped the team overcome the perception that they had to be on call 24/7." Once we were able to demonstrate that taking full days off (working 80%) was possible, the next challenge was whether people working full time could have predictable time off and still achieve similar benefits for themselves and the organization.

In our second experiment, we required each consultant to take one scheduled night off a week, during which he or she could not work after 6 PM—not even check or respond to e-mails or other messages. (This didn't mean that consultants were expected to work all other nights; rather, it meant they were to have one scheduled uninterrupted night off every week, no matter what was going on at work.) We again chose a challenging project: This team was working on a postmerger restructuring for a demanding client. The project required on-site interaction with members of the client organization in multiple locations, necessitating a great deal of overnight travel. But this time, we made no change in staffing.

Again, we met with resistance from the consultants, even though the time off in this experiment was outside the client's normal working hours. The general practice among consultants on the road is that they work very hard while away from home, but then they hope to have a reasonable day on Friday when they are back in the home office, and they want the weekends off. As a project manager summed up the skepticism surrounding the night-off experiment, "What good is a night off going to do? Won't it just force me to work more on weekends?"

In both experiments, participants felt conflicted between their commitment to the experiment and what they felt they owed both the client and their teammates. They were also concerned that involvement in the experiments wouldn't reflect well in their performance evaluations. As a consultant confided during the first week, "If you are making promotion decisions, and you look at someone who has been staffed on a project where she is really cranking it out and working long hours, and you compare that to someone who is getting a day off, it is hard to believe you are not going to promote the person who appears to be working harder."

As a result, consultants involved in the experiment worried that they were putting their careers in jeopardy. Moreover, they either worked and felt guilty, because they were in violation of the experiment, or they didn't work and felt guilty, because of the stress they thought they were putting on their teammates.

As time passed, their anxiety gradually subsided. Several weeks into the experiment, one consultant effused that his night off was phenomenal. "My project manager pushed me out of the office to make sure I took the time off," he said, "even though it was a busy week. I came back really refreshed." Before long, the consultants didn't need to be pushed into taking a little time for themselves.

In the five months following our initial experiments (which occurred in sequence over the course of a year), 10 more teams began experimenting with taking a night off. At the start of the experiments, participants were asked to rate the following statement: "I feel respected for setting boundaries." The scale ranged from 1 (strongly disagree) to 7 (strongly agree). In the first month, those on the experiment teams gave the statement a 3.7 ranking. In month five, they rated it at 5.2—demonstrating their slowly rising level of faith in the concept.

At the same time, 100% of people working on an experiment team and 76% of people in the rest of the office wanted their next case to be on a team experimenting with predictable time off. Compared with those not participating in the experiments, people on time-off teams reported higher job satisfaction, greater likelihood that they could imagine a long-term career at the firm, and higher satisfaction with work/life balance. (See figure 6-1.)

Beyond the intended work/life benefits, the participants reported more open communication, increased learning and development, and a better product delivered to the client. "It's a way to open up a conversation that everyone on your team wants to have, which is 'How

FIGURE 6-1

Early signs of progress

After only five months, consultants on teams experimenting with predictable time off perceived their work situations more favorably—on every dimension—than peers on nonexperiment teams. We asked consultants once a month to rate statements about their work situation on a scale of 1 (strongly disagree) to 7 (strongly agree). We saw statistically significant improvements across the board in the scores of teams that were scheduling regular days or nights off, demonstrating their growing faith in the time-off concept.

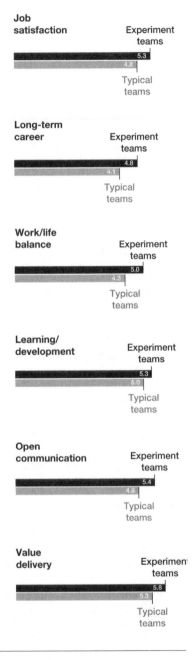

Job satisfaction

Experiment teams

5.3

4.8

Typical teams

Long-term career

Experiment teams

4.8

4.1

Typical teams

Work/life balance

Experiment teams

5.0

4.3

Typical teams

Learning/ development

Experiment teams

5.3

5.0

Typical teams

Open communication

Experiment teams

5.4

4.8

Typical teams

Value delivery

Experiment teams

5.8

5.3

Typical teams

can we work smarter? How can we work together more often, and how can we make sure we deliver without sacrificing work/life balance?'" one project manager told us. "The experiment not only allows you to talk more, but it forces you to do so weekly. In the end, the process creates efficiencies and promotes work/life balance—without sacrificing anything on the client side."

Let's look now at what enabled our experiments to deliver these benefits.

Lesson 1:
Impose a strict time-off mechanism

To get hard-driving consultants to agree to take time off during an assignment—not just when there happened to be a break in the work but at predictable times—we had to establish a mechanism that made it clear to everyone how time off must be taken: either a full day or a full night each week for everyone on the team, which was scheduled at the start of each project. All the team members knew for any given week which day or night they were to take off. Some teams opted to have each person take the same day or night each week (for instance, one team member had Monday, another had Tuesday, and so on). Other teams tried alternating the particular day or night off for each team member. On all teams, people spread out scheduled times off across the week to ensure coverage at work. Once the schedule was set, individuals were encouraged to make changes to accommodate personal events if they could do so without causing too much trouble for the team.

Admittedly, this arrangement didn't satisfy everyone. Some people in the day-off experiment, for example, would have preferred to come in late every morning instead. Most people would have preferred additional time off at home to a free night on the road.

Ultimately, the goal is for people to be able to take the type of time off that best suits their personal needs. To

UNPLUGGING FOR VACATION

We live in a world where we're expected to be available all the time, for almost any reason. Worse, we expect it from ourselves. While nonstop work might feel overwhelming, it's also reassuring. It makes us feel busy. Valuable. Indispensable.

So, leashed to our technology, we convince ourselves that we can't take a vacation that allows us to *really* get away.

We have two reasonable options for dealing with this problem:

1. **Completely unplug.** I've done this a few times, such as the week I spent camping and kayaking in the Grand Canyon. I was literally unreachable. When I returned to civilization—and a phone—I had more than 50 messages. But here's what's interesting: The first half of the messages raised problems that needed attention, and the second half were the same people telling me not to worry about their earlier messages because they had resolved the problems on their own.

get to that point, however, the feasibility of taking time off and the potential value of time off must first be recognized. Initially, everyone must take off the same type of time. Otherwise inequity (or the perception of it) can creep in. For example, is an hour in the morning the same as an hour at night? Is a Friday night off the same as a weeknight off? It quickly becomes quite complicated to assess

My unplugging created an opportunity for my team to grow, develop, and exercise their own judgment—and it gave me a wonderful, much-needed break.

2. **Schedule plug-ins.** If it's impossible or inappropriate to unplug completely, specify a time frame each evening when you'll be reachable—a few minutes at the end of each day (or, if you can manage, every few days) to answer e-mails and make phone calls. That sets clear expectations for the people trying to reach you, for the people you're vacationing with, and for yourself.

Of course, before you do this, you need to admit to yourself that you will work during the vacation. But by setting aside time to work, you're also setting aside the rest of the time *not* to work. And that just might save your vacation.

Adapted from content posted on hbr.org by Peter Bregman on March 18, 2010

the relative value of time off when it is freely selected. If everyone takes the same type of time off, people's fears that they aren't pulling their weight will be reduced. Team members will also be more attuned to protecting their own and their teammates' time off. And when the time off takes the same form for everyone, it's easier to track.

In the end, the people in our experiments generally managed to take their time off. In the first experiment, 90% of days off were taken in the designated week, and 68% were taken on the scheduled day (or another day when the change was solely for personal reasons). In the second experiment, 98% of nights were taken off in the designated week, and 86% were taken on the night scheduled (unless the change was solely for personal reasons). As a result, people came to recognize that the 24/7 mentality could be broken and began to appreciate the value of doing so.

Lesson 2:
Build dialogue into the process

In each of our experiments, we used explicit tactics to generate conversation around the time-off goals in particular, and around work processes more generally. The team began with a kickoff meeting in which the partners on the team emphasized the importance both of achieving the time-off goals and of team members' being open to and engaged in experimentation around work processes. After that, the teams had a weekly check-in to discuss how the experiment was going.

The check-ins consisted of three parts. One part involved a review of the calendar. Team members would discuss whether they had taken their time off as planned during the past week, and whether they expected to be able to take it in the week ahead. When people hadn't taken their time off or thought they wouldn't be able to, team members questioned one another about what was going wrong and how to improve the situation.

The second part involved a pulse check, where each person was asked to rate and talk about four questions: (1) How are you feeling? (2) How much value are you delivering to the client? (3) How satisfied are you with your learning? and (4) Is the current operating model sustainable for you throughout the project?

The third part of the check-ins was a discussion of "tummy rumbles"—items people submitted anonymously in advance, comprising anything that was making them uncomfortable.

The weekly check-ins resulted in a far greater emphasis on how work was being done than on what work was being done. As a project manager noted, "In a typical team meeting, you'd probably spend 95% of the time discussing the content, and maybe only 5% of the time actually looking at the process. Because of the experiment, we probably spent more like 30% of the time talking about the process, and 70% of the time on the content."

People were initially skeptical about spending so much time looking at work processes. But in the end, most teams found it helpful. The check-ins not only allowed teams to engage in explicit conversations about achieving their time-off goals, but they also sparked valuable discussions—involving the whole team—about priorities, expectations, and problems people were facing. By contrast, in typical, nonexperiment teams, consultants generally start talking about problems only when they are already overstressed and less able to think rationally or do much about them.

Our experiments emphasized open dialogue around a particular collective but personal goal: enabling individuals' time off. Because conversation was started on a focused, concrete topic, individuals could raise a small issue, see how it was received, and then choose whether to say more depending on the response. In the process, they gradually built trust and respect, enabling them to feel comfortable raising an increasingly wide range of topics. Team members learned about one another in more holistic ways, and they came to appreciate one another as human beings as well as business colleagues. And, in the end, they became all the more willing to speak up about their issues, both work-related and personal.

The discussions revealed not only small issues but large potential problems. "We were doing a major transformation piece, and the reaction from the client was critical for making it work," recalled one partner. "During an experiment check-in, consultants started raising concerns about the client's level of buy-in to our work. We came to realize that this was not an issue with just one member of the client organization; it was a pattern that each of the consultants was seeing in their contacts with the client." The team changed its approach accordingly, redoubling its efforts to get the client's buy-in.

Lesson 3: Encourage experimentation

Beyond creating a safe space for open dialogue, we found it imperative to encourage people to experiment with new work processes. Ways of working that would have previously gone unquestioned were suddenly fair game for reconsideration.

One core process that was called into question had to do with how team members' work was allocated. In management consulting, projects are typically done by teams, but the team leader usually divides the work among the team members, who have personal responsibility for their part of the project. To achieve the time-off goals—especially for a full day off when consultants had daily interactions with the client—this fundamental assumption about how work was done had to be revisited. New ways of "teaming," where individuals more closely shared responsibility for work and, therefore, could more easily cover for each other, were needed.

Various teams experimented with different ways of teaming. For instance, those in the day-off-a-week experiment tried assigning primary responsibility for each piece of work to one person but also allocating secondary responsibility to another one or two people. To ensure effective handoffs and hand-backs, this team instituted a team blog. Each evening, every member would post an account of the progress made on his or her own work—for example, progress made while covering for someone else, or even hallway conversations with clients that might have an impact on the work in general. This nightly report helped to break down the silos that usually kept people focused on their own work, and it elevated the discourse of the team as a whole.

Teaming let consultants share expected spikes in the workload and pitch in when demands arose unexpectedly. It also increased the exchange of knowledge and support among team members. "Think of all the times on cases you would love to grab another consultant for four hours, but you can't because they're so busy," one consultant explained. "Now people have more time for it because cooperation is built in." Consultants learned a great deal from one another as a result.

The work became better integrated because people were interacting better and more often. Inevitably, this led to improvements in the quality of work delivered—benefits that were certainly noticed by clients. As one noted, "This new way of working [gave BCG] a big advantage . . . [the consultants] were much more informed about what was going on with other modules, and people were more informed about the whole project."

Lesson 4:
Insist on leadership support

Individuals won't willingly engage in these experiments unless they are able to suspend their disbelief. For that to happen, people need to know that there is value in trying; that they will be respected for participating; and that they will bear some responsibility for the success or failure of the experiment.

One of the reasons we had such a high level of engagement from the consultants in our experiments was strong support from the senior partners. They set the tone, making it OK to talk about issues as they related to work and personal life.

Such legitimization, of course, required more than a few statements from the top brass. BCG's partners and project managers needed to model the desired openness.

For instance, the partners were encouraged to be more transparent when they were taking personal time. "It was helpful to know that the reason the partner missed a meeting was that he was taking his daughter on a college tour," one consultant noted. "That helped me see that these issues are important to him." Another consultant added that at a kickoff meeting, the senior partner said that work was very important to him but not the most important thing in his life, and he didn't want to have to be embarrassed to say so. The consultant reported, "I had never heard a partner talk like that before. My work is really important to me, too, but it is not the most important thing in my life. [His openness] made me comfortable to admit that."

Partners were required to attend the kickoff and weekly check-in meetings. It's often hard for a partner to prioritize spending time with the team when other important things, such as client meetings, are being postponed. But both the partners and the teams appreciated the increased involvement. As one partner put it, "A lot of these things, communicating with our teams, actually attending the team meetings—it's not that complicated, but it's easy to let them slide if you're not focused on them." Another partner added that the time-off experiments and the new processes brought him "closer to the content of the case than I've been in years."

To help the leadership team make these adjustments, we acted as facilitators during the first two experiments. We helped the partners understand the signals they were sending and encouraged them to support the experiments in both word and deed. We attended the weekly check-ins and followed up with each team member, to ensure that people were getting the support they needed to take their days or nights off and that team members were communicating openly with one another when issues arose.

During the next 10 time-off experiments, internal consultants at BCG were taken out of client service work to serve as full-time facilitators. They performed the same role we had in earlier experiments, attending weekly meetings, conducting regular check-ins, and prompting team members and BCG leaders to challenge assumptions and try new ways of working.

The Boston office of BCG, where the research originated, is now exploring changes in its formal reward system. It is piloting review forms for junior members of the firm that measure how well they communicate personal commitments and how well they plan and deliver against project needs while maintaining those personal commitments. It has also started to add questions to their upward-feedback forms to measure how well each senior member of the office models having a sustainable career and how well he or she respects the personal commitments of his or her teams.

Such explicit support for the predictable-time-off initiative provides a shield as the teams navigate between the firm's old norms and its new goals. A consultant who perceives unnecessary travel can raise the issue with his project manager by saying, for instance, "In the spirit of the time-off experiments, do we all really need to be on site at the client every day next week?" Once this question might have been seen as a lack of commitment at BCG; now it is safe, even encouraged, to question decisions about how work is done.

It's important to recognize that our experiments are not about reducing professionals' commitments to their work and clients. We understand that the success of professional services firms depends on hardworking people who value the intensity of the work and are committed to their clients. They relish being in the thick of things, with all the learning and adrenaline buzz that engenders. What professionals don't like is the bad intensity—having no control over their own work and lives, being afraid to ask questions that could help them better focus and prioritize, and generally operating in ways that are inefficient. Still, professionals accept the bad intensity without hesitation, believing it comes with the territory.

This only perpetuates a vicious cycle: Responsiveness breeds the need for more responsiveness. When people are "always on," responsiveness becomes ingrained in the way they work, expected by clients and partners, and even institutionalized in performance metrics. There is no impetus to explore whether the work actually requires 24/7 responsiveness; to the contrary, people just work harder and longer, without considering how they could work better. Yet, what we discovered is that the cycle of 24/7 responsiveness can be broken if people collectively challenge the mind-set. Furthermore, new ways of working can be found that benefit not just individuals but the organization, which gains in quality and efficiency—and, in the long run, experiences higher retention of more of its best people.

———————

Leslie A. Perlow is the Konosuke Matsushita Professor of Leadership at Harvard Business School in Boston. **Jessica L. Porter** is a research associate at Harvard Business School.

Chapter 7
Winning Support for Flexible Work

by Amy Gallo

Many professionals seek flexible work arrangements to accommodate lives that don't mesh with a 9-to-5 day. Yet few companies have official policies or programs for alternative schedules—and just as few managers are willing or equipped to provide them for members of their teams. This doesn't mean you should give up on the idea of flextime if it would help you cut down a lengthy commute or avoid burnout. It just means that the onus is on you to propose a plan that works for you, your boss, and your company.

What the Experts Say

Before you pursue a flexible schedule, recognize that you're likely to be bucking long-held conventions. "Tra-

---

Adapted from content posted on hbr.org on December 1, 2010

ditionally, managers were reluctant to have people work remotely because of lack of trust: Are you really working, or are you eating bonbons with your friend?" explains Stewart D. Friedman, founding director of the Wharton School's Work/Life Integration Project. Even those bosses who trust their employees worry about appearing to favor certain people or allowing productivity to decline.

Still, some managers and organizations are reaping the benefits of nontraditional schedules. Research from Lotte Bailyn, MIT management professor and coauthor of *Beyond Work-Family Balance*, shows that when employees have the flexibility they need, they meet goals more easily, they're absent or tardy less often, and their morale goes up. By focusing on these upsides and thoughtfully framing your request around them, you greatly increase your chances of getting approval for an alternative work arrangement.

Define What You Want

The first step is to figure out what you're trying to accomplish. Is your goal to spend more time with family? Less time at the office? Or do you want to remove distractions so you can focus on bigger, longer-term projects? Once you're clear on your goal, decide how you can achieve it while still doing your job effectively. Options include a compressed workweek, a job share, working from home, and taking a sabbatical. Of course, not every job is suited for a flexible arrangement. Before you make a proposal, think carefully about the impact your wished-for schedule will have on your boss, your team, and your performance.

Next, investigate what policies, if any, your company has and whether there's a precedent for flexibility. You won't need to blaze a trail if one already exists.

Design It as an Experiment

Many managers will hesitate to approve a flexible schedule, especially if your organization lacks established protocols. You can allay their fears by positioning your proposal as an experiment. "Include a trial period so your boss doesn't worry that things will fall apart," says Bailyn. "He or she needs to be able to see the new way of working."

In his book *Total Leadership: Be a Better Leader, Have a Richer Life,* Friedman talks about nine types of experiments you can do to gently introduce flexibility—everything from working remotely to delegating (see chapter 11, "Real Leaders Have Real Lives"). Whatever you propose, provide an out. Explain that if it doesn't work, you're willing to try a different arrangement or resume your former routine. "One can always go back to the original plan, but most such experiments work out very well," says Bailyn.

Ask for Team Input

"Our research has shown that flexibility only works when it's done collectively, not one-on-one between employee and employer," says Bailyn. Your team is affected by your work schedule, so you need everyone's support to make your new arrangement a success. Explain what you're trying to achieve and ask for their input. "Engage them in the planning," Bailyn says, and let your boss know that you've incorporated your colleagues' suggestions into your proposal.

Involving your team can help head off another common concern: Some bosses worry that if they grant one person flexibility, the floodgates will open and everyone will want the same arrangement. This is often an unfounded fear. Friedman points out that there's a difference between *equality* and *equity,* and, in fact, many people prefer a traditional schedule. "You don't give everyone the same thing because they don't *want* the same thing," he says.

Highlight the Benefits to the Organization

Emphasize the organizational benefits over the personal ones. "Whatever you try has to be designed very consciously to not just be about you or your family," Friedman says. "Instead, have the clear goal of improving your performance at work and making your boss successful." Demonstrate that you have considered the company's needs, that your new schedule will not be disruptive, and that it will actually have positive benefits, such as improving your productivity or increasing your relevant knowledge.

Reassess and Make Adjustments

Once your flexible schedule has been in place for three or four months, evaluate its success. Are you reaching your goals? Is the arrangement causing problems for anyone? Because you've designed it as a trial, you'll want to report back to your boss. "Get the data to support your productivity. Show that it's working," says Friedman. And if it's not, be prepared to suggest changes.

Case Study 1:
Creating a Unique Job Share

Julie Rocco was working as a program manager at Ford Motor Company when had she her first baby. She knew she wanted to return after her maternity leave, but she didn't see how she could work a 12-hour-a-day job and also be a hands-on mom. So she asked a mentor at Ford for advice. The answer? Take advantage of the company's commitment to flexible work by crafting a job that suited her. The mentor also suggested she talk to another Julie at Ford, Julie Levine, about job sharing. Levine, a mother of two, had shared a job before and wanted to try it again, not least because it would give her an opportunity to move into mainstream project development.

"It's very much like picking a spouse," Levine says of choosing the right job-share partner. "That person is your eyes and ears when you're not there." After checking each other out in what they now refer to as "a blind date," they agreed to pitch themselves as a pair to Ford's management. The plan was this: Each would work three days a week, overlapping one day—Rocco on Monday, Wednesday, and Thursday; Levine on Tuesday, Wednesday, and Friday. They opted against splitting the week in half to avoid "losing momentum" during long stretches away. Each evening, except for Wednesday, the person who'd been in the office would spend an hour and a half on the phone "downloading" the day's events to the one who'd been home. And on their days in common, they would either work together or, when things were exceptionally busy, divide and conquer. "It's our job to be seamless," they told their bosses. "We have the same outlook, the same goal, the same vision, the same work ethic. And you'll get more from us than one person could give."

"We said we would be a pilot," Levine recalls. Ford's management not only agreed, but also put the duo in charge of one of the company's highest-profile 2011 launches—the new Ford Explorer. The experiment was a success: Rocco and Levine are now known throughout the company as "the two Julies," twin dynamos. Both say the job share has made them happier at home and work, and also more effective. "One person might work a 12-hour day, go home and collapse, then have to do it all again the next day," Levine explains. "[With us], because you have to analyze your day and share it with another brain, [when] you show up the next day you're ready to run."

Case Study 2: Taking Time Off for Personal Development

Amit Desai had been working at Bayer Healthcare for 11 years when he decided he wanted to apply to Wharton's executive MBA program. However, his enrollment would mean attending a full day of school on Friday every other week and on an occasional Thursday for two years—more than 60 days away from his job as an automation project manager.

Although Bayer has official policies on telecommuting and flextime, special requests such as Desai's are decided on a case-by-case basis, so he was told to make a formal proposal. He started by looking into a similar request a previous employee had made and talking to his boss, who supported the plan with one stipulation: If a conflict ever arose, Desai would give priority to work over school. Desai agreed and created a pitch, including a detailed explanation of the MBA program and his goals in applying, a calendar of days he would be in school and how they tied into his work schedule, and a list of benefits to Bayer. "I have the ability to apply knowledge gained at school over the weekend to work on Monday," he told them. The vice president approved his request and wrote a letter endorsing his Wharton application.

Desai completed his MBA in 2011. Looking back, he says that the arrangement worked well because he was careful to coordinate with colleagues. Even though he was away from the office at set times, he reminded his immediate team when he would be out and blocked off the time in his Outlook calendar. "The stress level was low because my supervisor and peers always knew where I was," he says. And as he'd promised, he prioritized work over classes the few times that conflicts came up. He fulfilled his commitments at work while excelling in school.

———————

Amy Gallo is a contributing editor at *Harvard Business Review*. Follow her on Twitter: @amyegallo.

Chapter 8
How Two-Career Couples Stay Happy

by Jackie Coleman and John Coleman

More and more of us live in two-career households. Almost half of the married couples in the United States are dual-career, along with roughly 70% in Canada and around two-thirds in the United Kingdom. And these couples often struggle to balance work and home life.

We're part of that cohort, and we've had many discussions about what it means to manage a relationship and our careers. Being a former marriage counselor, Jackie has seen problems other couples face—determining who will drop everything to pick up a sick child at school, dividing the household chores, deciding whether to move

---

Adapted from content posted on hbr.org on July 27, 2012

for one partner's job, and so on. We've experienced those challenges and others, from living in different cities to coordinating crazy travel schedules. And because we each have unique needs and our own ideas about what we want from our jobs and home lives, we know that conversations about dual-career trade-offs can quickly become tense. But balance is possible, and you can thrive. The following tips will help you navigate the stresses of a two-career relationship.

Actively manage expectations

In relationships, unspoken assumptions often lead to disappointment and frustration. By clearly communicating those expectations up front, however, two-career couples can answer key questions before they cause tension. For example: How many meals should you eat together, and who will prepare (or buy) them? Who pays which bills? Do you need quiet time to decompress in the evening, or do you want to talk about the day's events with each other? Do you prefer frequent, brief interactions throughout the day (texts, instant messages, phone calls), or would you rather have lengthier conversations and more time together when you get home? How will you divide childcare responsibilities (drop-off and pickup, sick days, school vacation coverage)?

It's essential to have open and honest discussions about these things, but they won't always be smooth sailing. Neither person will get his or her way all the time. If you prefer one approach but your spouse or partner wants another, determine the areas in which you're able to be flexible. At each impasse, instead of focusing mainly on your needs, actively listen to your partner's preferences and concerns. The way you talk through these expectations and conflicts is extremely important. John Gottman, a leading researcher in marriage and relationships, says he can predict divorce with over 90% accuracy solely by analyzing how couples talk to each other in the first five minutes of an argument. And he has more than 35 years of data to back that up. While Gottman finds that the frequency of arguments is not a predictor of divorce, negative patterns like criticism and contempt are. Managing expectations through thoughtful discussion will help you argue constructively, not destructively.

Schedule time with each other

The average person spends 8.8 hours per day on the job—and for many of us, that number can double. To make sure everything gets done, we live by our calendars: We schedule meetings, reviews, time to complete tasks, trips to the gym, volunteer work, and breakfasts with friends. Most of us don't make appointments with our significant others, because we take it for granted that we'll see them. Research by Kingston and Nock, however, shows that one of the healthiest things you can do for your relationship is to put as much effort into booking time with each other as you do into managing your work schedules.

Recognizing that our professional obligations could theoretically take up all of our time, we've made a deliberate effort to schedule time together. Even with an infant at home, we commit to at least one date night per week, typically on Fridays. We regularly send each other Google calendar invitations for events we need to attend together or even uninterrupted time we'd like to spend with each other. Before we started doing this, we often forgot to communicate these requests effectively, leaving one or both of us frustrated and disappointed. But regular scheduling makes each of us feel prioritized by the other person and gives us time to look forward to each week. This keeps us happier at home and more relaxed at work.

Cheat on your job

Despite your best scheduling efforts, work can creep into your personal time. How many times has a meeting at the office conflicted with something you've scheduled at home? How often do you need "just a few hours" during evenings and weekends to catch up on e-mails or assignments? We often "cheat" on our families by putting in a few hours of work when we're at home; there should be corollary times when we cheat on our jobs. Try meeting occasionally for lunch or letting a scheduled date night trump an optional work event. Scheduling ensures that you spend time together—but spontaneity matters, too, and it can make these opportunities even more fun.

We work in different areas of town, but whenever Jackie's meetings are near John's office, she'll call to see if she can stop by to say a quick hello. Little gestures like this can make partners feel valued. And impromptu breaks from work for family may even improve work performance. Researchers say that willpower is like a muscle that can get fatigued—taking a quick breather from work can actually boost self-control and productivity on the job. With renewed focus at work, you can both manage your professional stress and keep your relationship fresh.

Integrate work and home

Dual-career relationships can become more difficult when work and home occupy completely separate spheres. Not knowing each other's colleagues can lead to feelings of alienation and disconnectedness. You might feel out of touch with each other's day-to-day concerns, for example, or not understand inside jokes from work. Or it can be more serious than that: In an informal Vault.com survey, 32% of respondents reported having an "office spouse," a coworker with whom one has an intimate (nonphysical) relationship. These intimacies can sometimes cross a line. In her practice of more than 20 years, marriage and family therapist Shirley Glass found that 46% of unfaithful wives and 62% of unfaithful husbands had an affair with someone at work.

Even if cheating isn't an issue, you and your partner may be uncomfortable with each other's long nights at the office, business trips, and bonds with unknown colleagues. To avoid this, find ways to introduce your colleagues and your partner (or your family more broadly). Plan occasional dinners after work and encourage your coworkers to bring their spouses. Share anecdotes about your day and your coworkers with your significant other. Attend work-related social events together. These are just some ways in which you can build trust with your partner *and* humanize and deepen your professional relationships.

Share the compromises

Compromise is essential to healthy two-career couples, but sometimes it falls too consistently on one person. It's quite common when children arrive, for example, for one partner (often a woman) to forgo career ambitions while the other gives up time at home. If one person sacrifices more—or even feels that way—frustration and resentment can build. There's no one-size-fits-all solution here, but by speaking frankly about how much of the load you each feel you're shouldering, you can prevent one person from making all the concessions.

Some big questions to consider: Whose job should you relocate for? Whose family will you live closer to? Does one partner feel responsible for supporting the family financially while the other has more flexibility to pursue what he or she wants, regardless of financial benefit? Who will bear primary child-rearing responsibility? If you look back over a catalog of these decisions and one partner is consistently sacrificing for the other, it might be time to assess whether that's what you as a couple intended or whether someone is feeling undervalued. Even small compromises add up: Whose family do you visit on which holidays? Who does which household chores? Periodically track these things for a week or two or simply discuss them to make sure the relationship really is a partnership—with decisions and compromises shared fairly.

Reassess

Just like a year-end review at work, regularly carve out time to assess your relationship and your priorities as individuals and as a couple. Keep the lines of communication open and adapt your plans as needed. How are things going? If your spouse or partner could change something, what would it be? Do you both feel connected? What's working well? Overall, how is your partner feeling? Asking questions like these shows that you're making the relationship a high priority. And that will help you manage dual-career stress and can keep things on track at work *and* at home.

Jackie Coleman is a former marriage counselor and currently works on education programs for the State of Georgia. **John Coleman**, her husband, is a coauthor of *Passion & Purpose: Stories from the Best and Brightest Young Business Leaders* (Harvard Business Review Press, 2011). Follow him on Twitter: @johnwcoleman.

Chapter 9
Don't Take a Bad Day Home with You

by John Baldoni

Feeling frustrated at work—especially late in the day, when you're worn out? Right before you go home, do something that comes easily to you.

That advice was given to my daughter, a drop-in diver in a collegiate program. One day she had hit a wall and was about to head home when her coach pulled her aside and said, "Instead of leaving in a state of frustration, why don't you finish practice with a dive you *know* you do well?" My daughter followed her suggestion and left feeling much better about herself and her abilities.

Adapted from content posted on hbr.org on August 9, 2010

And that's exactly what we nondivers need to do. Things inevitably go wrong on the job because of our own or others' mistakes or failed systems or processes. Whatever the cause, tension builds. To prevent that stress from following you out the door and ruining your evening, dissipate it before you wrap things up.

Whether it's sending off a routine report or replying to a few straightforward e-mails, cross an item off your to-do list. Pick something that doesn't require much thought. This type of activity tends to slow your heart rate and give you a sense of ownership of what you're doing.

Once you've completed the task—and are hopefully feeling better—exit promptly. Do not check your e-mail one last time. Do not linger to see who else is hanging around. Just leave—gracefully, and with a smile on your face. The onerous work will be there tomorrow, but for the moment, flush it from your memory. For now, just go.

Of course, this won't always work. Sometimes you'll still leave exasperated. And if that happens more often than not, you probably have a larger problem to solve. You may need to find a new position, a new employer, or even a new line of work. But for the occasional bad day, doing one more dive that makes you feel good about yourself before you head home can help you leave your frustrations behind you.

John Baldoni is a leadership consultant, coach, and speaker. His newest book is *The Leader's Pocket Guide* (AMACOM, 2012).

Section 4
Finding the Tools That Work for You

Chapter 10
Positive Intelligence

by Shawn Achor

In July 2010 Burt's Bees, a personal-care products company, was undergoing enormous change as it began a global expansion into 19 new countries. In this kind of high-pressure situation, many leaders pester their deputies with frequent meetings or flood their in-boxes with urgent demands. In doing so, managers jack up everyone's anxiety level, which activates the portion of the brain that processes threats—the amygdala—and steals resources from the prefrontal cortex, which is responsible for effective problem solving.

Burt's Bees's then-CEO, John Replogle, took a different tack. Each day, he'd send out an e-mail praising a team member for work related to the global rollout.

Reprinted from *Harvard Business Review*, January–February 2012 (product #R1201G)

He'd interrupt his own presentations on the launch to remind his managers to talk with their teams about the company's values. He asked me to facilitate a three-hour session with employees on happiness in the midst of the expansion effort. As one member of the senior team told me a year later, Replogle's emphasis on fostering positive leadership kept his managers engaged and cohesive as they successfully made the transition to a global company.

That outcome shouldn't surprise us. Research shows that when people work with a positive mind-set, performance on nearly every level—productivity, creativity, engagement—improves. Yet happiness is perhaps the most misunderstood driver of performance. For one, most people believe that success precedes happiness. "Once I get a promotion, I'll be happy," they think. Or, "Once I hit my sales target, I'll feel great." But because success is a moving target—as soon as you hit your target, you raise it again—the happiness that results from success is fleeting.

In fact, it works the other way around: People who cultivate a positive mind-set perform better in the face of challenge. I call this the "happiness advantage"—every business outcome shows improvement when the brain is positive. I've observed this effect in my role as a researcher and lecturer in 48 countries on the connection between employee happiness and success. And I'm not alone: In a meta-analysis of 225 academic studies, researchers Sonja Lyubomirsky, Laura King, and Ed Diener found strong evidence of directional causality between life satisfaction and successful business outcomes.

Another common misconception is that our genetics, our environment, or a combination of the two determines how happy we are. To be sure, both factors have an impact. But one's general sense of well-being is surprisingly malleable. The habits you cultivate, the way you interact with coworkers, how you think about stress—all these can be managed to increase your happiness and your chances of success.

Develop New Habits

Training your brain to be positive is not so different from training your muscles at the gym. Recent research on neuroplasticity—the ability of the brain to change even in adulthood—reveals that as you develop new habits, you rewire the brain.

Engaging in one brief positive exercise every day for as little as three weeks can have a lasting impact, my research suggests. For instance, in December 2008, just before the worst tax season in decades, I worked with tax managers at KPMG in New York and New Jersey to see if I could help them become happier. (I am an optimistic person, clearly.) I asked them to choose one of five activities that correlate with positive change:

- Jot down three things they were grateful for.

- Write a positive message to someone in their social support network.

- Meditate at their desk for two minutes.

- Exercise for 10 minutes.

- Take two minutes to describe in a journal the most meaningful experience of the past 24 hours.

The participants performed their activity every day for three weeks. Several days after the training concluded, we evaluated both the participants and a control group to determine their general sense of well-being. How engaged were they? Were they depressed? On every metric, the experimental group's scores were significantly higher than the control group's. When we tested both groups again, four months later, the experimental group still showed significantly higher scores in optimism and life satisfaction. In fact, participants' mean score on the life satisfaction scale—a metric widely accepted to be one

HAPPINESS AND THE BOTTOM LINE

For companies, happy employees mean better bottom-line results. Employees who score low in "life satisfaction," a rigorously tested and widely accepted metric, stay home an average of 1.25 more days a month, a 2008 study by Gallup Healthways shows. That translates into a decrease in productivity of 15 days a year.

In a study of service departments, Jennifer George and Kenneth Bettenhausen found that employees who score high in life satisfaction are significantly more likely to receive high ratings from customers. In addition, researchers at Gallup found that retail stores that scored higher on employee life satisfaction generated $21 more in earnings per square foot of space than the other stores, adding $32 million in additional profits for the whole chain.

of the greatest predictors of productivity and happiness at work—moved from 22.96 on a 35-point scale before the training to 27.23 four months later, a significant increase. Just one quick exercise a day kept these tax managers happier for months after the training program had ended. Happiness had become habitual. (See the sidebar "Happiness and the Bottom Line.")

Help Your Coworkers

Of the five activities described above, the most effective may be engaging positively with people in your social support network. Strong social support correlates with an astonishing number of desirable outcomes. For instance, research by Julianne Holt-Lunstad, Timothy Smith, and Bradley Layton shows that high levels of social support predict longevity as reliably as regular exercise does, and low social support is as damaging as high blood pressure.

The benefits of social support are not just physical. In a study of 1,648 students at Harvard that I conducted with Phil Stone and Tal Ben-Shahar, we found that social support was the greatest predictor of happiness during periods of high stress. In fact, the correlation between happiness and Zimet's social support scale (the academic measure we used to assess students' positive engagement with their social networks) was a whopping .71—for comparison, the correlation between smoking and cancer is .37.

That study focused on how much social support the students *received*. But in follow-on research I conducted in March 2011, I found that even more important to sustained happiness and engagement was the amount

THE PERFORMANCE CONNECTION

- In a sweeping meta-analysis of 225 academic studies, Sonja Lyubomirsky, Laura King, and Ed Diener found that happy employees have, on average, 31% higher productivity; their sales are 37% higher; their creativity is three times higher.

- My research shows that employees who score the highest on providing social support are 40% more likely to receive a promotion in the following year, report significantly higher job satisfaction, and feel 10 times more engaged by their jobs than people who score in the lowest quartile.

of social support the students *provided*. For example, how often does a student help others when they are overwhelmed with work? How often does he initiate social interactions on the job? Social support providers— people who picked up slack for others, invited coworkers to lunch, and organized office activities—were not only 10 times more likely to be engaged at work than those who kept to themselves; they were 40% more likely to get a promotion.

How does social support work in practice as a tool for employee happiness? Ochsner Health System, a large health care provider that I work with, uses an approach it calls the "10/5 Way" to increase social support among employees and patients. We educated 11,000 employees, leaders, and physicians about the impact of social support on the patient experience, and asked them to modify their behavior. When employees walk within 10 feet of another person in the hospital, they must make eye contact and smile. When they walk within 5 feet, they must say hello. Since the introduction of 10/5, Ochsner has experienced an increase in unique patient visits, a 5% increase in patients' likelihood to recommend the organization, and a significant improvement in medical-practice provider scores. Social support appears to lead to not only happier employees but also more-satisfied clients.

Change Your Relationship with Stress

Stress is another central factor contributing to people's happiness at work. Many companies offer training on how to mitigate stress, focusing on its negative health effects. The problem is, people then get stressed-out about being stressed-out.

It's important to remember that stress has an upside. When I was working with Pfizer in February 2011, I asked senior managers to list the five experiences that most shaped who they are today. Nearly all the experiences they wrote down involved great stress—after all, few people grow on vacation. Pick any biography and you'll see the same thing: Stress is not just an obstacle to growth; it can be the fuel for it.

Your attitude toward stress can dramatically change how it affects you. In a study Alia Crum, Peter Salovey, and I conducted at UBS in the midst of the banking crisis and massive restructuring, we asked managers to watch one of two videos, the first depicting stress as debilitating to performance and the second detailing the ways in which stress enhances the human brain and body. When we evaluated the employees six weeks later, we found that the individuals who had viewed the "enhancing" video scored higher on the Stress Mindset Scale—that is, they saw stress as enhancing, rather than diminishing, their performance. And those participants experienced a significant drop in health problems and a significant increase in happiness at work.

Stress is an inevitable part of work. The next time you're feeling overwhelmed, try this exercise: Make a list of the stresses you're under. Place them into two groups—the ones you can control (like a project or your in-box) and those you can't (the stock market, housing prices). Choose one stress that you can control and come up with a small, concrete step you can take to reduce it. In this way you can nudge your brain back to a positive—and productive—mind-set.

It's clear that increasing your happiness improves your chances of success. Developing new habits, nurturing your coworkers, and thinking positively about stress are good ways to start.

———————

Shawn Achor is the CEO of Good Think and the author of *The Happiness Advantage* (Crown Business, 2010).

Chapter 11
Real Leaders Have Real Lives

by Stewart D. Friedman

You can be a committed "A" player executive, a good parent, an attentive spouse, and a healthy person with time for community engagement *and* hobbies. How on earth do you do all that? Stop juggling and start integrating. Begin with a clear view of what you want from—and can contribute to—each domain of your life (work, home, community, and self). Carefully consider the people who matter most to you and the expectations you have for one another. Then experiment with some minor changes and see how they affect all four domains over a short period. If an experiment doesn't work out in one or more areas,

---

Adapted from "Be a Better Leader, Have a Richer Life," *Harvard Business Review*, April 2008 (product #R0804H) and content posted on hbr.org on February 21, 2013

you make adjustments or put an end to it, and little is lost. But if it does work out, it's a small win. Rack up enough small wins, and you're well on your way to a life that's less stressful and more productive.

Skeptical? Many people are when they first hear about this approach. But time and again, I've seen maxed-out professionals use it to find the greater harmony they're seeking.

To show what it looks like in practice, I'll share a couple of stories from Target executives who have experimented their way toward improving their well-being and performance.

Manage Boundaries

David is a VP accountable for a multibillion-dollar P&L. (All names and titles are disguised.) For years, he felt a relentless tension between the domains of work and home, as many of us do. "I spent most of my waking hours at work," he explains, "and I always shut down from work at home." But keeping things separate like this hurt his relationship with his wife. They talked about the kids, nothing more, because that was all they had in common. And at work, David never had enough time to prepare for all his meetings.

So he devised an experiment. Before leaving the office each day, he'd look at the next day's schedule and pick one big meeting to get ready for. On his drive home—at a decent hour—he'd think about what he could do and say at that meeting. When he got home, he'd run some ideas by his wife.

It worked beautifully: "This gave us something new to talk about each day, it gave her a much better understanding of what I do, it engaged her, and it enhanced our relationship because we were having richer conversations. My wife made good suggestions—and I've had better meetings as a result."

The experiment has also had a positive effect on David's team. After he told his direct reports he was changing his hours in the office, one of them approached him with a request to adjust *her* schedule, because it was aggravating a medical problem. Another employee said he felt empowered to take care of an aging parent during the day when he needed to. He didn't feel guilty about it—David's own actions made it clear that it was OK.

"The example I was setting before was work first, work first, work first," David reflects. "Now I might be in the office for fewer hours, but I'm making faster and better decisions. And my wife has more understanding when work does have to come first. In the long term, this means that I'm a more engaged leader for Target without an unmanageable tension between my wife and my work."

Be the Change

Changing old run-yourself-ragged norms isn't easy. But by modeling new behavior, senior executives at Target are accelerating a "well-being" movement in the organization.

Take Max, who now runs the company's largest P&L business. He admits he "saw a couple of eyebrows raised" when he first told his team that he would come in late two mornings a week so he could "go to the gym and have breakfast with my kids." Max adopted this schedule as an experiment. He's kept it up because it's effective: He's more closely connected to his family, and it's noticeably improving his focus and performance at work.

David (from earlier) also finds this to be true. His boss supports his experiments and asks for regular updates on them. "She's also given me tips and shared what she's learned in her experience," he says. "I talk to her about all this to hold myself accountable. She's reminded me that each new job in my career will be bigger and more demanding, so it's critical to get better and better about managing my commitments as I continue to develop."

When senior leaders in an organization take highly visible steps to reduce stress *and* improve performance— as David, Max, and their managers have done—more and more employees feel free to generate experiments of their own. Slowly, the culture changes. People at all levels discover that it makes good business sense to take care of all the things that matter in their lives.

Pursue Four-Way Wins

The most fruitful experiments help you make improvements across the four domains. At work, you may want to increase productivity or reduce hidden costs. Goals for home and community may include strengthening relationships and contributing more to social causes. For self, they're usually about becoming healthier and finding greater meaning in life.

How can a single experiment help you check off several—or all—of the boxes in table 11-1? Some experiments improve one domain directly and others indirectly. For example, being more disciplined about your diet will have a direct impact on your health, but it may also give you more energy for your work and help you handle stress better, which in turn might make you a better parent and friend. Other activities—such as running a half-marathon with your kids to raise funds for a charity sponsored by your company—will feed all four domains simultaneously. Whether the benefits are direct or indirect, achieving a four-way win is the goal. That's what makes the changes sustainable: Everyone gains. Keep in mind that some benefits may be subtle or delayed—far-off

TABLE 11-1

Where are you feeling the most pain?

Before you can design smart experiments to better integrate the four domains of your life, you'll need to figure out what's most important to you and identify your biggest pain points. Using a four-way chart will help you set your priorities. I've filled out a sample one here, based on a fictitious professional we'll call Joan, but you can find a blank worksheet and other tools at www.totalleadership.org.

	Importance	Focus	Satisfaction 1=not at all satisfied 10=fully satisfied
Work	20%	70%	1 2 3 4 5 ⑥ 7 8 9 10
Home	40%	20%	1 2 ③ 4 5 6 7 8 9 10
Community	15%	0%	① 2 3 4 5 6 7 8 9 10
Self	25%	10%	1 ② 3 4 5 6 7 8 9 10
Overall	100%	100%	1 2 3 ④ 5 6 7 8 9 10

Joan's reflection: I have to admit that what my husband says is true: I spend most of my time either at work or working from home. We don't do anything together anymore, except take care of the kids. We're losing touch as a couple. Also, I'm feeling tired and out of shape, even though my health is important to me. I do think my job and family are more important than community stuff, but it surprises me to realize I'm doing nothing in that area. Maybe I could do something active with my husband that would help me and our relationship—and even benefit the community.

career advancements, for instance, or a contact who might ultimately offer valuable connections.

Pace Yourself—and Gauge Your Progress

It's not practical to try out more than three experiments at once. (Typically, two turn out to be relatively successful and one goes haywire.) So after you've brainstormed lots of possibilities, narrow down the list to the three options that will:

- Give you the best overall return on your investment

- Cost the most in regret and missed opportunities if you *don't* do them

- Allow you to practice the leadership skills you most want to develop

- Involve more of what you enjoy doing

- Move you closest to your vision of how you want to lead your life

Once you begin experimenting, however, don't become too wedded to the details of any one plan. You will at some point need to make adjustments.

The only way to fail with an experiment is to fail to learn from it, which makes useful metrics essential (see table 11-2). No doubt it's better to achieve results than to fall short, but failed experiments give you, and those around you, information that helps create better ones in the future.

TABLE 11-2

Experiment worksheet

Suppose that Joan, the hypothetical professional described in table 11-1, has decided to try exercising three mornings a week with her spouse to address the pain points she identified in her four-way chart. In the sample worksheet below, she spells out her experiment's goals and tracks her progress in achieving them.

As you implement your own experiments, you may find that your initial goals or metrics are too broad or vague, so refine your scorecard as you go to make it more useful. The main point is to have practical ways of measuring your progress.

Experiment: Exercise three mornings a week with my husband.

Life area	Experiment's goals	How I will measure success	Implementation steps
Work	Improving alertness and productivity	No caffeine to get through the day, better morale on my team, more productive sales calls	• Get doctor's feedback on exercise plan • Join gym • Set alarm earlier on exercise days • Tell coworkers, family, and friends about my plan, how I need their help, and how it will benefit them
Home	Spending more time with husband	Fewer arguments, feeling closer	
Community	Increasing strength to participate in athletic fundraising events with friends	Three 10K fundraising walks completed within a year	
Self	Improving self-esteem	Greater confidence	

For a blank version of this worksheet and other tools, go to www.totalleadership.org.

Depending on your goals, your metrics may include cost savings from reduced travel, number of e-mail misunderstandings averted, degree of satisfaction with family time, hours spent volunteering at a teen center, and so on. They can be objective or subjective, qualitative or quantitative, reported by you or by others, and frequently or intermittently observed.

Highly ambitious experiments usually fail because they're too much to handle. When the stakes are smaller, it's easier to overcome the fear of failure that inhibits change—and you open doors that would otherwise be closed. You can say to your stakeholders, "Let's just try this. If it doesn't work, we'll go back to the old way or try something different." People who will be affected by the change will be more receptive if they know it's not permanent and if they have a say in whether it's working according to *their* expectations.

Stewart D. Friedman is Practice Professor of Management at the Wharton School. Formerly the head of Ford Motor's Leadership Development Center, he is the author of *Total Leadership: Be a Better Leader, Have a Richer Life* (Harvard Business Review Press, 2008). Follow him on Twitter: @StewFriedman.

Chapter 12

A Practical Plan for When You Feel Overwhelmed

by Peter Bregman

We've all experienced it: that feeling that we've got so much to do that there's no chance we'll get it all done. And certainly not done on time. Right now, I'm feeling completely overwhelmed by my to-do list.

Here's the crazy part. I just spent the last two days *trying* to work without actually working. I start something but get distracted by the internet. Or a phone call. Or an e-mail. At a time when I need to be most efficient, I've become less efficient than ever.

You'd think it would be the opposite—that when we have a lot to do, we'd become very productive in order to get it done. Sometimes that happens.

Adapted from content posted on hbr.org on September 23, 2010

But often, when there's so much competing for our attention, we don't know where to begin—so we don't begin anywhere.

Next time you find yourself in this situation, try this approach:

1. **Write down everything you have to do on a piece of paper.** Resist the urge to use technology for this task. Why? I'm not sure, but somehow writing on paper—and then crossing things out—creates momentum.

2. **Spend 15 minutes completing as many of the easiest, fastest tasks on your list as you can.** Make your quick phone calls. Send your short e-mails. Don't worry about whether these are the most important tasks on your list. You're moving. The goal is to cross off as many tasks as possible in the shortest time. Use a timer to keep you focused.

3. **Work on the most daunting task for the next 35 minutes without interruption.** Turn off your phone, close all the unnecessary windows on your computer, and choose the most challenging task on your list, the one that instills the most stress or is the highest priority. *Then work on it and only it*—without hesitation or distraction—for 35 minutes.

4. **Take a break for 10 minutes, then begin the cycle again.** After 35 minutes of focused work, take

a break. Then start the hourlong process over again, beginning with the 15 minutes of quick actions.

"Thirty years ago," Anne Lamott writes in her book *Bird by Bird*, "my older brother, who was 10 years old at the time, was trying to get a report on birds written that he'd had three months to write. It was due the next day. We were out at our family cabin in Bolinas, and he was at the kitchen table close to tears, surrounded by binder paper and pencils and unopened books on birds, immobilized by the hugeness of the task ahead. Then my father sat down beside him, put his arm around my brother's shoulder, and said, 'Bird by bird, buddy. Just take it bird by bird.'"

That's it. *Bird by bird, starting with a bunch of easy birds to help you feel accomplished and then tackling a hard one to gain serious traction and reduce your stress level.* All timed.

Working within a specific and limited time frame is important because the **race against time keeps you focused**. When stress is generalized and diffuse, it's hard to manage. Using a short time frame actually increases the pressure but keeps your effort specific and particular to a single task. That increases good, motivating stress while reducing negative, disconcerting stress. So the fog of feeling overwhelmed dissipates, and forward movement becomes possible.

In practice, I'm finding that although I make myself work at least the full 35 minutes, I don't *always* stop when the 35 minutes of hard work are over, because I'm in the middle of something and I have traction. On the other hand, though it's tempting, I don't exceed the 15 minutes of easy, fast work. When the timer stops, so do I, immediately transitioning to the hard work.

Maybe this method has been working simply because it's novel for me and, like a new diet, offers some structure to motivate my effort. Today, though, it doesn't matter, because it's a useful tool for me. And I'll keep using it until I don't need it or it stops working.

Am I still stressed? Sure. But overwhelmed? Much less so. Because I'm crossing things off my list and getting somewhere on my little tasks as well as my big ones, bird by bird.

———————

Peter Bregman is a strategic adviser to CEOs and their leadership teams. His latest book is *18 Minutes: Find Your Focus, Master Distraction, and Get the Right Things Done* (Business Plus, 2012).

Chapter 13
Desk Yoga

6 Poses You Won't Be Embarrassed to Do—Even in an Open Environment

by Linda Steinberg

Many of us sit behind our desks and stare at computer screens for far too much of the day. Although concentrated work can be beneficial to our jobs, it can be taxing on our bodies. The following yoga exercises will help you relieve any tension you might feel after too many hours of poring over spreadsheets. The poses also provide long-term benefits with regular practice. Each pose takes fewer than two minutes to complete, and you can do the whole series in just 10 minutes—but I promise you'll feel the effects long after.

Breathe deeply throughout the poses because sending oxygen to your muscles allows them to relax.

Shoulder Rolls (2 minutes)

- Sitting upright, lift your right shoulder to your ear. Slowly roll your shoulder around and back, dropping it away from your ear.
- Lift your left shoulder to your ear. Slowly roll your shoulder around and back, dropping it away from your ear.
- Continue these rolls three more times, alternating right and left.
- Lift both shoulders up to your ears and hold for a breath. Release them, slowly rolling your shoulders around and back, dropping them away from your ear. Repeat five times and then relax your shoulders.

Open Chest Stretch (1 minute)

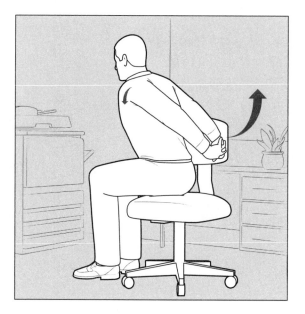

- Sit near the edge of your chair and interlace your fingers behind you, palms together and facing your back.
- Lean forward slightly, lifting your arms so that you feel the stretch in your chest.
- Inhale slowly, lifting your chest.
- Exhale and relax your shoulders away from your ears.
- Hold for 10 to 15 breaths.
- Slowly release your hands and return them to your sides.

Neck Stretch (1 minute)

- Sit upright without letting your back touch the back of the chair.
- Hold your head directly over your spine, as if there is a string lifting the crown of your head up.
- Drop your right ear toward your right shoulder without lifting your right shoulder or turning your head.
- Take several breaths in and out, feeling the stretch on the left side of your neck.
- To create a deeper stretch, reach your right hand over your head and place it on the left side of your face. Hold the pose for at least five more breaths and then release your hand and straighten your neck, gently massaging your neck and shoulders with your left hand.
- Repeat on your left side.

Chair Twist (2 minutes)

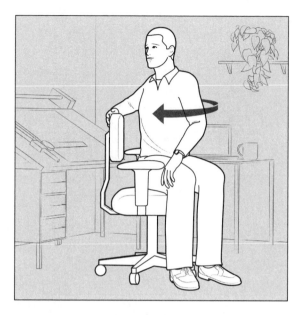

- Sit near the edge of the chair, but turn your thighs toward the right side of the chair so that you are sitting diagonally. If you have an armrest on the side of your chair, bring your thighs as close to it as possible.
- Move your arm to the back of the chair on the opposite side, taking hold of the chair back with your right hand. With your left hand, take hold of your right knee or armrest.
- Breathe deeply, focusing on lengthening your spine.
- Twist to the right, pressing your right hand against the back of the chair to deepen the stretch. Focus on drawing your shoulder blades down.
- Breathe deeply, completely filling and emptying your lungs. Hold the pose for 10 to 15 breaths.
- Return to the center.
- Repeat on your left side.

Reverse Prayer Pose (2 minutes)

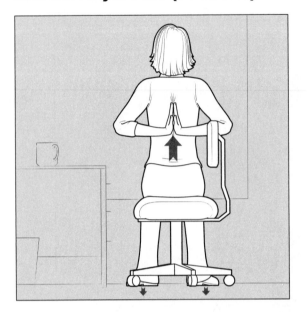

- Sit near the edge of your chair. Reach your arms around behind you and bring your palms together, fingertips pointing down.
- Rotate your wrists and turn your fingertips in toward your spine until your fingertips are pointing up.
- Slide your palms back together in prayer position.
- Use one hand to help pull the other hand up further on your back, to a comfortable spot. Be sure your shoulders are straight, not rounded.
- Press the outside edges of your palms lightly into your back. Press your palms together gently.
- Press your feet into the floor.
- Breathe deeply, completely filling and emptying your lungs. Hold the pose for 10 to 15 breaths.
- Exhale and release your arms.

Twisted Arms (2 minutes)

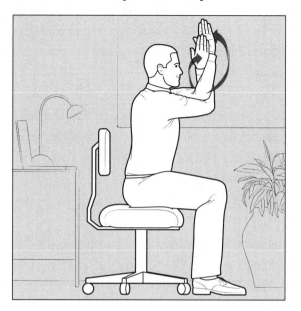

- Sit upright without letting your back touch the back of the chair.
- Reach your arms out in front of you at shoulder level.
- Tuck your right elbow into the crook of your left arm, and curl your forearms up into a 90-degree angle. The backs of your hands will be against each other.
- If you can, place your left fingers on your right palm, keeping palms straight in a single line with your nose.
- Breathe deeply, completely filling and emptying your lungs. Hold the pose for 10–15 breaths.
- Return to the center.

(*continued*)

(*continued*)

- Tuck your left elbow into the crook of your right arm, and curl your forearms up into a 90-degree angle. The backs of your hands will be against each other.
- If you can, place your right fingers on your left palm, keeping palms straight in a single line with your nose.
- Breathe deeply, completely filling and emptying your lungs. Hold the pose for 10 to 15 breaths.
- Exhale and return to the center.

Linda Steinberg is a certified yoga instructor who has been practicing and teaching partner-assisted yoga for over 20 years. Learn more about her work at www.yoga tothetenth.com.

Chapter 14
Diversify Yourself

by Peter Bregman

Suicides account for almost one-third of U.S. work-related deaths caused by violence. It's tempting to blame companies for driving their employees too hard and failing to handle people with care, compassion, and respect. But the problem is deeper and more complicated than callous management teams who care about nothing except profits. The problem is also in how *we* as professionals see and define ourselves.

Often the first question we ask when we meet someone is, "What do you do?" We have become our work, our professions. Connected 24/7 via mobile devices, obsessively checking e-mail and voice mails, we have left no space for other parts of ourselves.

If we spend all our time working, traveling to work, planning to work, thinking about work, or communicating

Adapted from content posted on hbr.org on October 21, 2009

about work, then we will see ourselves as workers and nothing more. As long as work is going well, we can survive that way.

But when we lose our jobs, or fear that we might, our very existence is put into question. "Establishing your identity through work alone can restrict your sense of self and make you vulnerable to depression, loss of self-worth, and loss of purpose when the work is threatened," says Dr. Paul Rosenfield, assistant clinical professor of psychiatry at Columbia University.

Who am I if you take away my work? That's a question to which we'd better have a solid answer. Fortunately, once we realize this, we can do something about it.

We can diversify.

I don't mean diversifying your money, though that's a good idea, too. I mean diversifying *yourself* so that when one identity fails, the other ones keep you alive. If you lose your job but you identify passionately as a mother or a father, you'll be fine. If you have a strong religious identity or view yourself as an artist, you'll be fine.

Here's the thing, though: It's not enough to *see* yourself in a certain way; you need to *act* on it. It won't help if you identify as a father but rarely spend time with your children. Or if religion is a big part of your identity and yet you rarely engage in religious activities.

Cultivating multiple identities will help you perform better in each one, because you learn things as an athlete or a parent or a poet that will make you a better employee or leader. And if you believe that doing nothing but work is necessary to support your lifestyle, then it's worth look-

ing at ways to change your lifestyle, so you don't kill yourself trying to maintain it.

Walk away from e-mail and have dinner with your
family. Leave work at a decent hour and play tennis with
a friend. Choose nonwork rituals that have meaning to
you (see also chapter 3, "Manage Your Energy, Not Your
Time"). Doing the same thing repeatedly over time so-
lidifies your identity.

When a good friend of mine lost her job, I called to see
if I could do anything. My intention was to help her find
a new job as soon as possible; I knew money was tight.

I was pleasantly surprised, though. She told me she
had decided to postpone her job search for a few months.
She was pregnant and wanted to focus on that for a while.
Once she felt ready, she would look for work. She was too
busy creating an identity as a mother to get caught up in
her identity as a worker.

Recently I received an e-mail from her telling me she
was back at work. "I love the job," she told me. "It's a great
balance to motherhood."

————————

Peter Bregman helps CEOs and their leadership teams
break down silos and tackle their most important priorities together. His latest book is *18 Minutes: Find
Your Focus, Master Distraction, and Get the Right
Things Done* (Business Plus, 2011). He can be reached at
www.peterbregman.com.

Index

Index

Notes

Notes

Notes

Notes

Notes

Notes

Notes

Smart advice and inspiration from a source you trust.

Whether you need help tackling today's most urgent work challenge or shaping your organization's strategy for the future, *Harvard Business Review* has got you covered.

HBR Guides Series

HOW-TO ESSENTIALS FROM LEADING EXPERTS

HBR Guide to Better Business Writing
HBR Guide to Finance Basics for Managers
HBR Guide to Getting the Right Work Done
HBR Guide to Managing Up and Across
HBR Guide to Persuasive Presentations
HBR Guide to Project Management

HBR's 10 Must Reads Series

IF YOU READ NOTHING ELSE, READ THESE DEFINITIVE ARTICLES FROM HARVARD BUSINESS REVIEW

HBR's 10 Must Reads on Change Management
HBR's 10 Must Reads on Leadership
HBR's 10 Must Reads on Managing People
HBR's 10 Must Reads on Managing Yourself
HBR's 10 Must Reads on Strategy
HBR's 10 Must Reads: The Essentials